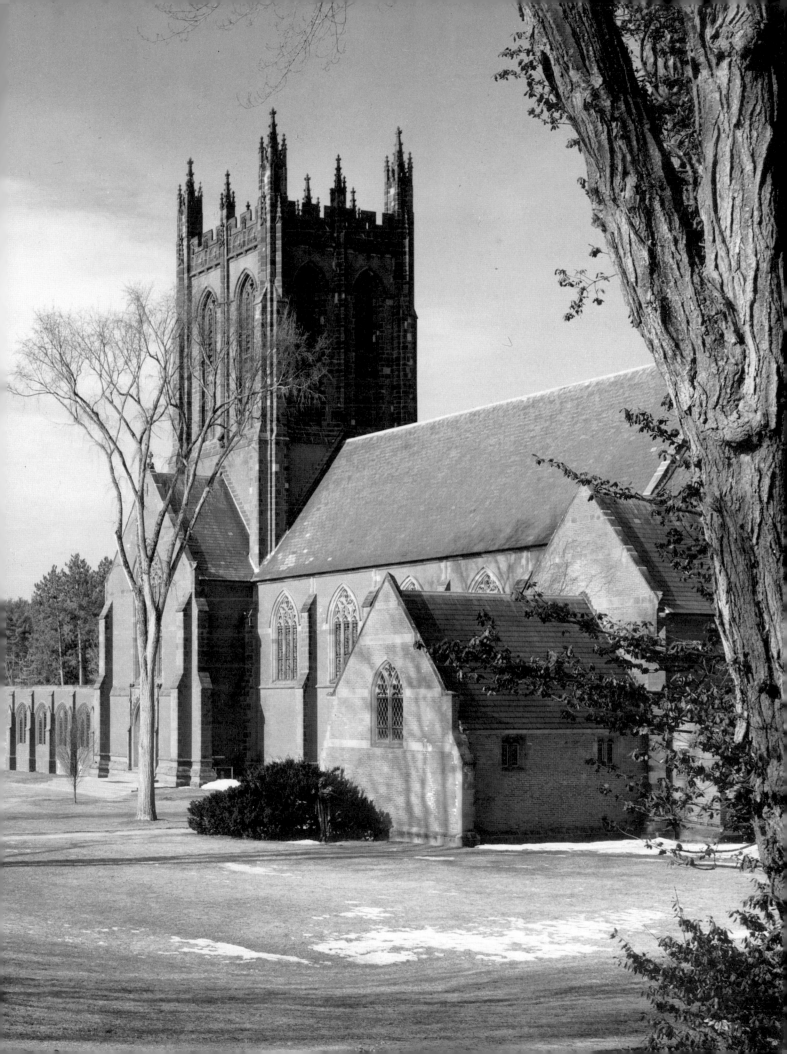

ROBERT A. M. STERN

ROBERT A. M. STERN

Buildings and Projects
1987-1992

Introduction by Vincent Scully

Edited by Elizabeth Kraft

RIZZOLI
NEW YORK

First published in the United States of
America in 1992 by
Rizzoli International Publications, Inc.
300 Park Avenue South
New York, New York 10010

Library of Congress Cataloguing-in-
Publication Data
Robert A. M. Stern, buildings and projects,
1987–1992 / introducton by Vincent Scully.
p.   cm.
Includes bibliographical references.
ISBN 0-8478-1618-4
ISBN 0-8478-1619-2 (pbk.)
1. Stern, Robert A. M.—Criticism and
interpretation.   2. Architecture, Modern—
20th century—United States.   I. Stern,
Robert A. M.   II. Scully, Vincent Joseph,
1920–
NA737.S64R63   1992   92-18367
720'.92—dc20   CIP

Front cover: Skyview, Aspen, Colorado,
1987–90. Photo: Robert Reck, Courtesy of
Architectural Digest. © 1992. All rights
reserved.

Back cover and frontispiece: Ohrstrom
Library, St. Paul's School, Concord, New
Hampshire, 1987–91. Photos: © Peter
Aaron/ESTO.

Designed by Abigail Sturges
Rizzoli Editor: Kate Norment

Printed and bound in Japan

Acknowledgments

For this book, the third in a series documenting my work 9
and that of my partners, associates, and colleagues practicing
architecture as Robert A. M. Stern Architects, I am indebted
to the continuing support of Gianfranco Monacelli and the
staff at Rizzoli, most especially David Morton. Abigail
Sturges deserves special thanks for her elegant book design.
Kate Norment's copyediting was invaluable. Randy Correll
of our office contributed to the editorial effort, as did
Adonica Inzer and, especially, John Saunders, who prepared
most of the line drawings in the book.

The photographs of Peter Aaron, Steven Brooke, and
Timothy Hursley are indispensable and inspired documents
of our completed work. John Mason and Andrew Zega's
watercolor drawings are also essential documents, marking
key stages of a project's development from initial sketch to
reality.

Vincent Scully has been characteristically deep-seeing and
direct in his introductory assessment. Elizabeth Kraft has
been thorough, efficient, tactful, and imaginative in
organizing and editing the volume.

Robert A. M. Stern
July 1992

Contents

Biography

Robert A. M. Stern was born on May 23, 1939, in New York City. After receiving a B.A. degree from Columbia University in 1960, he received his Master of Architecture degree from Yale University in 1965. Stern began his professional career as the first J. Clawson Mills Fellow of the Architectural League of New York. In 1966 he worked in the office of Richard Meier, and from 1967 to 1970 he was a special assistant for design in the Housing and Development Administration of the City of New York. In 1969 he and John Hagmann established Stern & Hagmann Architects, a partnership that lasted until 1977, when the firm became Robert A. M. Stern Architects. In 1988 Stern formed a partnership with Robert S. Buford, Jr., and in 1989 Roger H. Seifter, Paul L. Whalen, and Graham S. Wyatt joined the partnership.

An educator and writer as well as a practicing architect, Stern is a professor at the Graduate School of Architecture, Planning, and Preservation at Columbia University and presently the director of its program in historic preservation. From 1984 to 1988 he served as the first director of Columbia's Temple Hoyne Buell Center for the Study of American Architecture. Stern has been associated with the Institute for Architecture and Urban Studies, and from 1973 to 1977 he was president of the Architectural League of New York. He has lectured extensively in the United States and abroad and is the author of numerous articles and books. During the period covered by this monograph, Stern, with Thomas Mellins and Gregory Gilmartin, was the author of *New York 1930* (Rizzoli, 1987) and, with Raymond Gastil, of *Modern Classicism* (London: Thames & Hudson; New York: Rizzoli, 1988). In 1986 he hosted "Pride of Place: Building the American Dream," an eight-part, eight-hour documentary television series on American architecture aired on the Public Broadcasting System.

Over its twenty-three-year history, Robert A. M. Stern Architects has earned international recognition and numerous awards and citations for design excellence, including National Honor Awards of the American Institute of Architects in 1980, 1985, 1990, and 1991. A Fellow of the American Institute of Architects, Stern received the Medal of Honor of its New York Chapter in 1984.

The work of Robert A. M. Stern Architects has been exhibited at numerous galleries and universities and is in the permanent collections of the Museum of Modern Art, the Metropolitan Museum of Art, the Deutsches Architekturmuseum, the Denver Museum of Art, and the Art Institute of Chicago. In 1982 Stern was the subject of a one-man exhibition at the Neuberger Museum of the State University of New York at Purchase. In 1980 he designed the section devoted to the 1970s in the Forum Design Exhibition held in Linz, Austria. In 1976 and 1980 he was among the architects selected to represent the United States at the Venice Biennale. During the period covered by this monograph, a number of books devoted to Stern's work have been published: *Robert A.M. Stern: Modernità e Tradizione*, edited by Lucia Funari (Rome: Edizioni Kappa, 1990), with an introduction by Paolo Portoghesi; *Robert A.M. Stern: Selected Works* (London: Academy Editions, 1991); and *The American Houses of Robert A.M. Stern*, with an introduction by Clive Aslet (New York: Rizzoli, 1991).

Introduction

Vincent Scully

I believe that Robert A. M. Stern's recent architecture has come to speak for itself. Its purpose and effects are perfectly clear, fully formed, and no longer require extensive introduction.

It is true that Stern has set himself the task of learning how to design and build as a traditional architect who can handle traditional styles of architectural form in an efficiently eclectic manner. He and his office as a whole have worked hard for many years to learn to work properly in many architectural modes, employing wholly convincing details. Stern therefore feels free to choose the style that seems best suited to the job at hand and to the context in relation to which it is to be seen. So a building by him for St. Paul's School will be of a very different style than one intended for Tokyo. St. Paul's loving nineteenth-century Romanesque/Gothic will be matched by a good wallop of nineteenth-century Hungarian nationalism in the American Embassy in Budapest and a solid shot of early twentieth-century Georgian in Boston and a heavy dose of Shingle Style in Orlando and Marne-la-Vallée and a fine slice of Jefferson, much filtered through the Yale Divinity School, in Charlottesville itself.

For this reason one would not expect that the concept of a personal style would be so important to Stern as it was to Frank Lloyd Wright or indeed to any of the modern masters of the past generation. In other words, Stern, unlike those masters, is theoretically not trying to create an original style of his own. He had the wit to put that dream away in his youth after some spectacular disasters befell him. And he knows that modern architecture as a whole has suffered from too much of that self-centered attitudinizing in the recent past. Despite all that, I think that Stern has now at last created a style of his own in fact. Each of his later buildings, whether a Shingle Style or classical country house or 222 Berkeley Street in Boston or the embassy in Budapest or a Euro Disney hotel, Western or Shingle Style, in the suburbs of Paris, bears his special stamp—one not difficult to distinguish or describe. It comes across as something foursquare, blunt, at once forthright and rather lush, not very subtle, perhaps a bit on the brutal side. There is also a kind of rich, vulgar imagery in it, or a perception of what may be done with that imagery, which may be distressing at times but is perhaps one of its greatest strengths. So Stern at first adapted the suffocating attributes of the typical shelter book interior—all those plump cushions—and then almost entirely recast them into something much more spatial and powerful without vitiating their fatty aura, and he now seems more capable than any other architect of embodying Disney's popular fantasies in appropriate architectural forms, and with a kind of rough wit absent from his earlier work.

It might be argued that those qualities derive naturally enough from Stern's own realistic, emotionally tough, rather impatient conceptual stance, but they reflect his specific historical interests as well, especially those in the classicism of the late nineteenth and early twentieth centuries. That classicism itself was pretty tough and often rather marvelously vulgar. Therefore, because he knows and values Japanese classicizing architecture as it took shape during its early Westernizing days, Stern's buildings in Japan (especially the Bancho House in Tokyo) are to me much more typically modern Japanese than those of other very distinguished Western architects working in Japan, such as Aldo Rossi and Frank Gehry. Stern's Bancho House is heavy-limbed, heavy-handed, massive, and brooding. It has the quality—shared by many modern Japanese buildings of whatever style—of resembling nothing so much as a battleship of the Kongo class wallowing in the water, with top-heavy upper works, primitive and dangerous. The classicism of Edwardian England—another great naval power of the dreadnought era?—has many of the same qualities. If somewhat less violent in effect, it is often at least as massively aggressive and florid, and Stern knows and values it well.

Indeed Stern's greatest quality, whether as architect or critic, has always been his ability—a very rare one—to perceive what exists, not to twist phenomena to his perceptions but to *see* them, to recognize them as they are. Philip Johnson, in a sense Stern's most immediate role model, shares this gift. But Stern has perhaps worked harder at devising a kind of consistent architectural expression from it. So he will never fall back into the easy abstraction of modernism as Johnson has done. He is in the real modern world for keeps and is himself a formidable exemplar of some of its major qualities. He knows the good. His library for St. Paul's may be his best building and is surely his most gentle, with beautiful space, beautifully sited. But good or bad, Stern sees what is around us—sickening luxury, brutal power, prepackaged proletarian dreams, whatever it may be—and he perceives it with a wondering, ravished, agate eye and builds, somehow, with it. One is sometimes surprised to find that Europeans seem to prefer his work to that of some other American architects who may appear to us to be more original or to design with more complexity, tension, or finesse than he. One has heard Europeans call his work "more accessible" than theirs. And this may well reflect a perception on their part of its curious authenticity as an expression of ourselves and an embodiment of today's dominant realities. History may find them right. Certainly there are going to be enough buildings by Stern standing around the world to give history a good shot at judging them fairly.

Buildings and Projects, 1987–1992

Robert A. M. Stern
Architects Office

New York, New York
1985

1. *View into west drafting room*
2. *Reception area*
3. *Principal partner's office*
4. *Floor plan*
5. *View from library into west drafting room*

18   This fourteen-foot-high loft space is enclosed on three sides by a large band of industrial sash that provides sweeping views of the Hudson River.

A principal axis of movement was created to form a sequence that is a metaphor both for a house and for the firm's design process. The reception and exhibition area in the Ionic order is the most formal space, leading into a library—the heart of the plan, as it is of the firm's design approach—and then to the principal partner's office, which sits at the edge, opening onto the two drafting rooms and to the city and river beyond.

In order to heighten the contrast between the existing fabric and the architects' interventions, the window walls and ceiling of the loft were not repainted. The two open studio spaces are presided over by super-scale "table" lamps in the Doric order that provide ambient illumination.

1

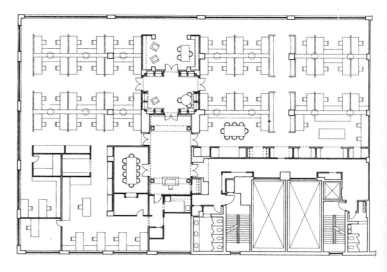

2

3

4

0 6 12   24 ft

Apartment House,
Fan Pier Development

Boston, Massachusetts
1986

20 This twenty-one-story, 160-unit apartment house was to be part of a large waterfront development facing Boston Harbor directly across from downtown and backing up on a newly created residential and commercial center. The semicircular plan of the building responds to the fan shape of the pier on which it is sited, maximizing waterfront exposure for a majority of the apartment units along the proposed canal. The base of the building consists of shops and loftlike studio apartments; facing the water, the base is formed by duplex maisonettes that harbor private gardens in the space between the units. Setbacks on the upper floors create private terraces leading to two top floors, where duplex apartments enjoy attic space lit by traditional dormers.

1

2

3

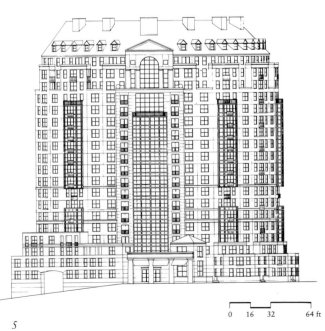

4

5

0 16 32   64 ft

Residence at Lily Pond Lane

East Hampton, New York
1983–85; 1988

1. *Approach to house*
2. *View from tennis court and terrace garden*
3. *View from northeast*
4. *View from beach*

22 Designed by Roger Bullard in 1924 and altered by Grosvenor Atterbury in 1927, this house had undergone little change for more than fifty years. Inside, it reflected a previous era when many servants were employed and many houseguests were accommodated, creating the need for a series of small bedrooms and baths. In renovating the house, many of these rooms were eliminated to create larger bedrooms and to permit higher ceilings in some rooms.

Outside, little was done to alter the mountainous shingled roofs and their strong silhouette at the top of the bluff. But a series of round windows was added, one at the center of each major axis of the house—east, west, and south—and flat-roofed dormers were replaced with hipped-roof dormers, which echoed the larger hipped roof of the house. A new swimming pool is enclosed by a colonnade of massive stucco columns that support a large lattice fence. In 1988 a tennis court and a terrace garden were added for new owners.

1

2

3

24

NORTH ELEVATION

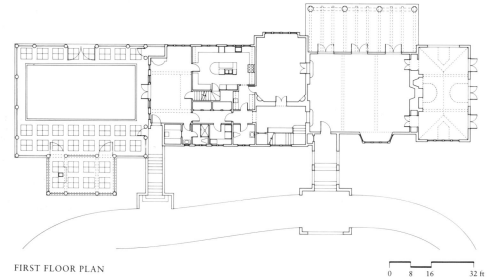

FIRST FLOOR PLAN

0   8   16   32 ft

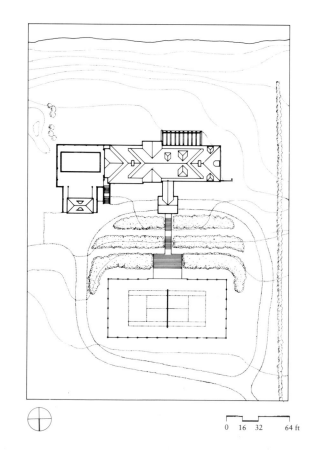

SITE PLAN

0   16   32   64 ft

6

7

8

Residence

Brooklyn, New York
1983–86

26   This single-family detached house occupies what was the only undeveloped lot in a neighborhood largely constructed in the 1920s. The design attempts to refine the architectural themes that typify the neighboring houses and to establish a unique identity through the quality and character of its detailing and the rich mixture of its materials. The basement and first floor are rusticated with alternating bands of red brick and granite, while the second floor is faced with cream-colored stucco. Painted steel casement windows and a hipped roof with green-glazed tiles complete the vocabulary.

Rooms are gathered about an entry hall that rises two floors through the house and culminates in a gilt dome. Although the rooms are constricted in size, they appear larger because of their generous twelve-foot ceilings and their arrangement along an axis that allows for the visual "borrowing" of space from adjacent hallways.

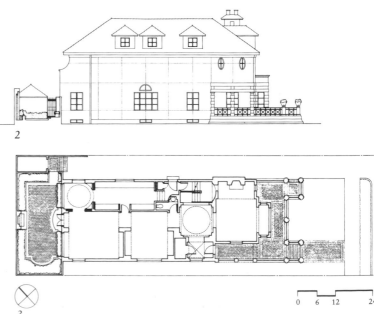

1

2

3

0   6   12   24 ft

4

5

6

7

Apartment Tower, Union Theological Seminary Claremont Tower, Manhattan School of Music

New York, New York
1986, 1987

1. *Claremont Tower, view from south*
2. *Context photo from southwest showing both sites*
3. *Union Theological tower, perspective view looking northwest from Broadway and 120th Street*
4. *Site plan indicating both tower sites*
5. *Union Theological tower, west quadrangle elevation*

28   In attempting to help the Union Theological Seminary take advantage of its unused air rights, the firm proposed a thirty-nine-story, 345-unit apartment tower to be located at the northeast corner of the seminary's Gothic quadrangle, created by Allen and Collens in the first decade of the twentieth century. To moderate the impact of this substantial intervention, our 400-foot-tall tower would have risen in part from a base made up of the existing buildings, much as the Harkness Tower rises from Branford College at Yale. The base of our building would continue the detailing of the existing quadrangle facades, and a new cloister arcade would link it with the seminary social hall. This would have reconfigured the somewhat casually organized courtyard into two intimately scaled, interrelated but separate spaces, with proportions closely resembling those proposed by the three finalist schemes of the 1907 competition for selection of an architect for the seminary.

In 1987, when the seminary decided not to proceed, an alternate strategy was proposed, wherein the adjacent Manhattan School of Music on Claremont Avenue would expand on a vacant lot to its north, allowing a four-story addition to the music school to slip in under a thirty-four-story residential tower. The school's portion of the building contains a library, technical support space for the school's opera stage, music practice rooms, and dormitory space. The apartment tower, which has its own entrance on a quiet residential street, contains approximately 265 apartments, a health club, and underground parking for 120 cars. The design of the brick music tower draws strongly from the existing school building's watery classicism, as well as from the far more robust Grant's Tomb, located a block to the west across Sakura Park. To emphasize the continuity between new and old, the tower rises from a rusticated limestone base that continues that of the existing school. In addition to providing expanded space for the school, the building exerts a strong presence in the architecturally rich and eclectic Morningside Heights area.

1

2

3

4

RIVERSIDE DRIVE

SAKURA PARK

CLAREMONT AVENUE

W. 120TH

W. 122ND

BROADWAY

0   80   160   320 ft

5

0   32   64   128 ft

Copperflagg Corporation Residential Development

Staten Island, New York
1983–89

30   The goal of this project was twofold: to invest a speculative suburban development with architectural coherence and dignity, and to work sensitively within the delicate context of a designated landmark district. The site is part of the former estate of Ernest Flagg, the great Beaux-Arts–trained architect best known for designing the Singer Tower in New York, the Corcoran Library in Washington, D.C., and the United States Naval Academy in Annapolis. Flagg erected his own Dutch Colonial–style mansion at the edge of the site, on the highest point of Staten Island, and surrounded it with outbuildings and small suburban houses, which he intended to be exemplars of a standardized system of construction that would become a model for future developers, and which he published in his 1922 book, *Small Houses: Their Economical Design and Construction.*

There were two phases to the development. Along the approach to the mansion, where the issues of contextualism are especially critical, a number of existing French Norman outbuildings were interwoven with new houses, in the spirit of Flagg's designs, to surround a formal garden located in the basin of an abandoned swimming pool. On the remainder of the site, prospective owners were encouraged to build unique houses under stylistic guidelines developed by the firm. In addition to the new houses in the French Norman village, the firm designed five other houses on the property.

1. *View of garden and French Norman village looking southeast*
2. *Site plan*
3. *Palm House, view into courtyard*
4. *Perspective of development*

1

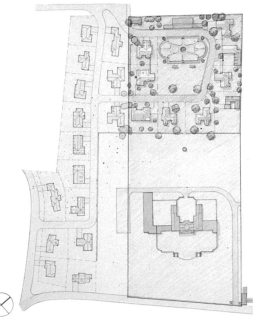

2

0   60 120   240 ft

3

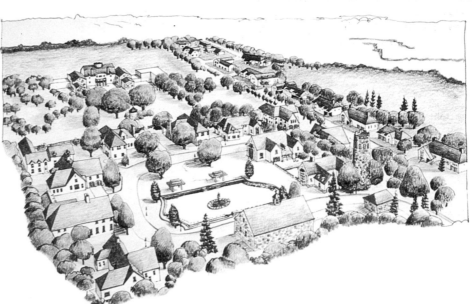

4

32

5

6

7

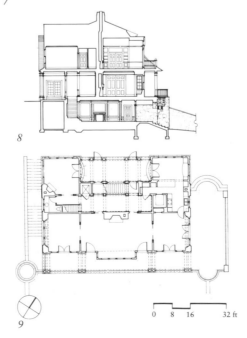

8

9

0   8   16   32 ft

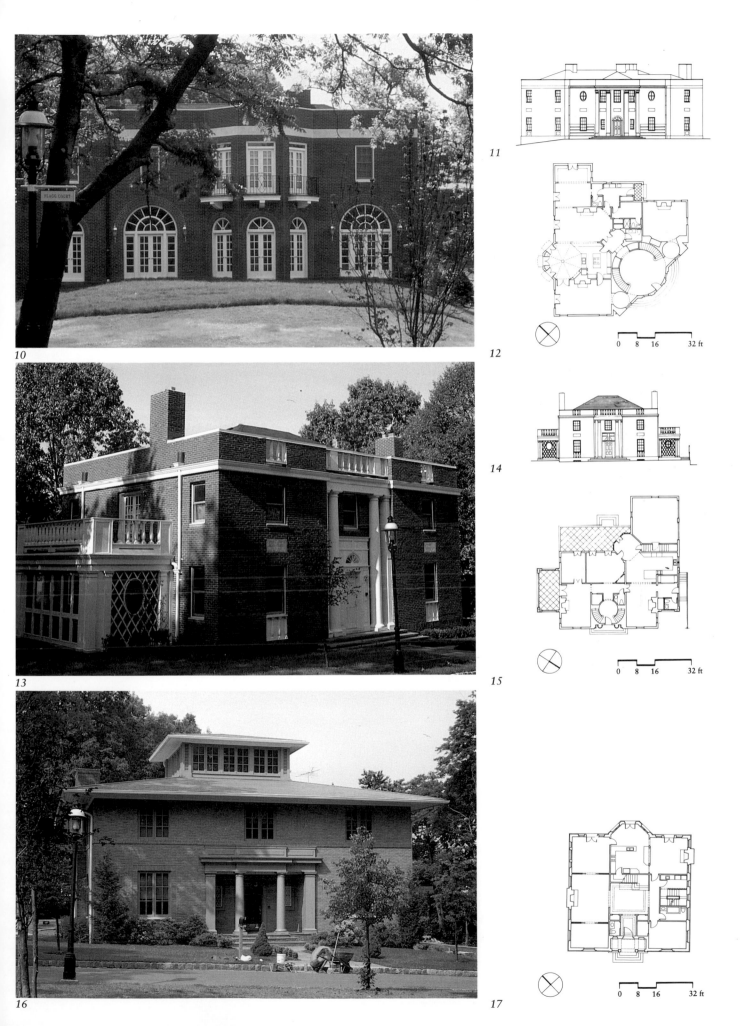

10

11

12

13

14

15

16

17

33

Villa in New Jersey

1983–89

34 Located among turn-of-the-century Italianate villas of an established resort colony, this house explores the integration of architecture with an idealized, classical landscape. House and garden are revealed gradually. From the street only a narrow facade can be glimpsed through a gate. The driveway circles beneath a porte cochere, where a garden wall conceals the service court. A vestibule leads past a long hall to an enfilade combining card, living, and dining rooms, each opening up to a pergola-shaded terrace that overlooks a sunken court. Framed by telescoping walls and low trees, a vista of grass terraces forms a cross-axis stretching from the house toward a carved limestone fountain basin in the distance. Beneath the pergola terrace, a grottolike indoor poolroom receives the axis of the sunken court and its forced perspective.

At the western end of the house are the more informal living spaces. The breakfast room overlooks a small orchard and the outdoor pool; the double-height family room commands the axis of a flower garden leading to the garden's secret room, created by a yew hedge.

1

2

3

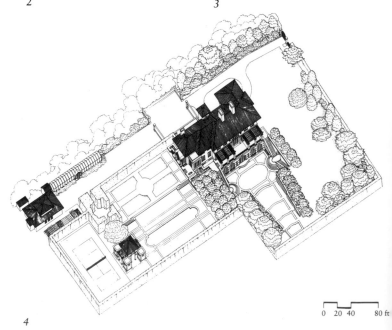

4

0　20　40　　80 ft

5

6

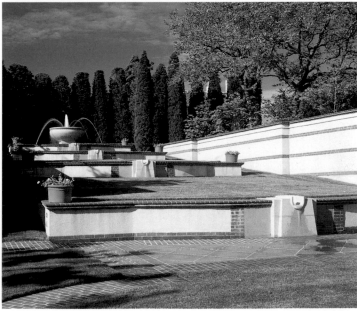

7

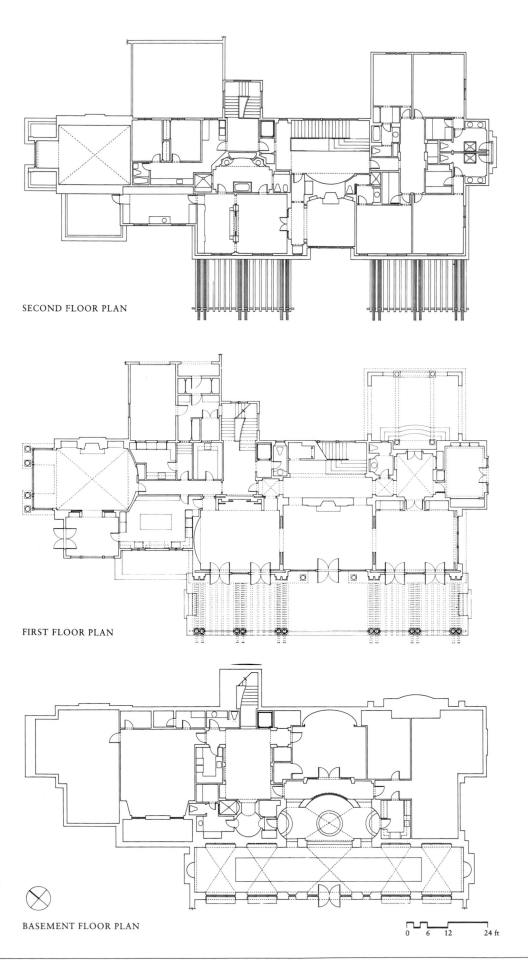

SECOND FLOOR PLAN

FIRST FLOOR PLAN

BASEMENT FLOOR PLAN

0   6   12   24 ft

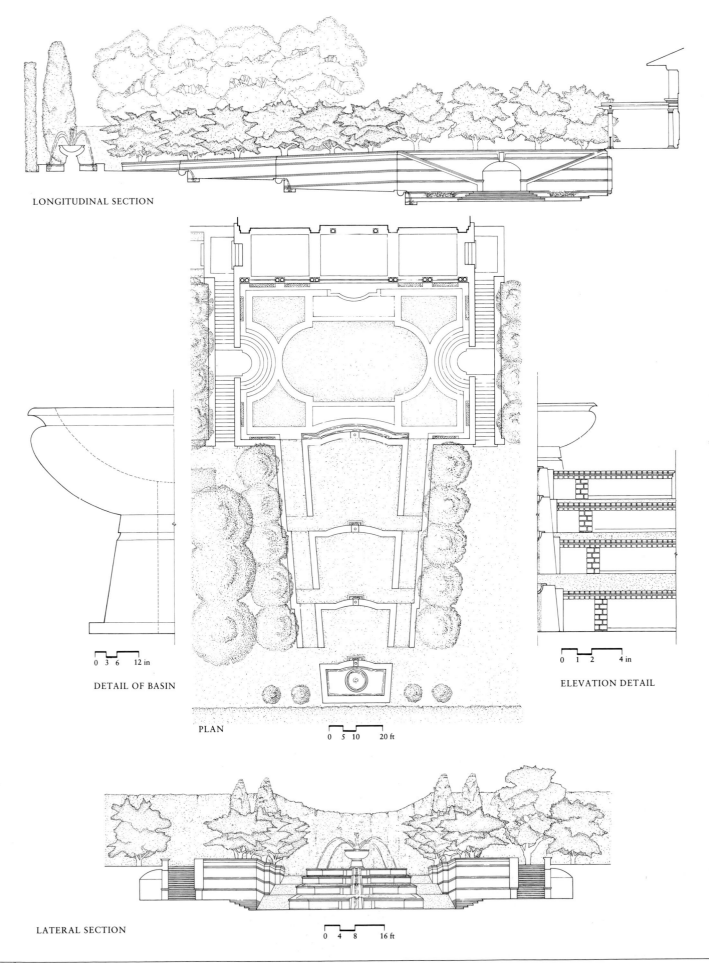

LONGITUDINAL SECTION

DETAIL OF BASIN

0 3 6   12 in

PLAN

0 5 10   20 ft

ELEVATION DETAIL

0 1 2   4 in

LATERAL SECTION

0 4 8   16 ft

38

10

11

12

13

14

15

16

17

0   3   6   12 ft

0   2   4   8 ft

0   1   2 ft

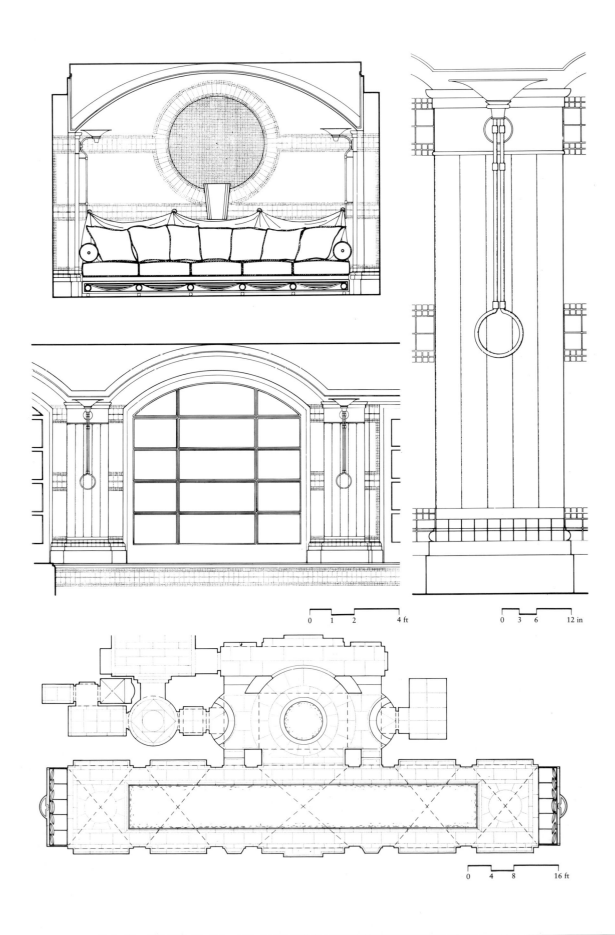

0 1 2   4 ft

0 3 6   12 in

0 4 8   16 ft

42

23

20. *View toward outdoor pool*
21. *Pergola*
22. *View from southwest*
23. *Pool pavilion*
24. *View from formal garden*

20

21

22

Residence

Marblehead, Massachusetts
1984–87

44 Set on a steeply pitched site with northern views toward the water, this house continues the tradition of the stone and timber cottages that have dotted Boston's North Shore as well as the rest of coastal New England since the late nineteenth century. As the land falls away, a rubble-stone foundation emerges to form a high base anchoring the more finely detailed and picturesquely massed shingled superstructure. Responsive as it is to the sometimes conflicting requirements for good interior planning, solar orientation, and view, the massing of the house—replete with projecting bays and subsumed porches—is rendered formally sensible by a complex network of hipped roofs rising hierarchically to a unifying ridge line.

An L-shaped plan makes the house appear more compact when viewed from the beach; at the front, this configuration defines an entry precinct separated by high garden walls from a service court. Within the house, planning centers about the interwoven planes and volumes of the cruciform living room, double-height entry hall, and turreted stair.

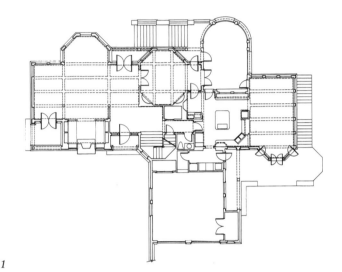

1

2

0 4 8   16 ft

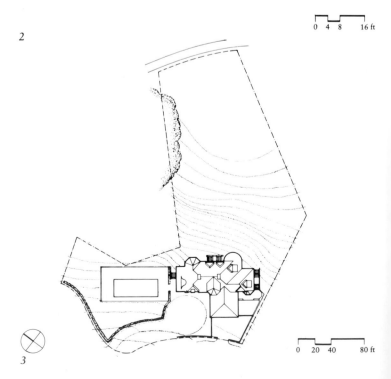

3

0   20   40   80 ft

4

5

6

7

Sunstone

Quogue, New York
1984–87

46 The two-story lighthouselike tower at the southwest corner of this house provides the living room and master bedroom with a panoramic view of Shinnecock Bay. The large gambreled roof sweeps down over the verandas that encircle the house and afford the interior rooms comforting shade from the summer sun. The main roof mass is punctuated by a variety of dormer types and engages the smaller, subordinate roofs of the garage and the screened porch. The entry facade combines the vernacular gambrel with a classical entry portico and Palladian stair-hall window.

Inside the entry hall is a generous room that forms the heart of the first-floor plan: it leads to the reception room, library, living room, dining room, and staircase to the second floor. Upstairs, the master-bedroom suite is raised above the level of the rest of the second floor to enhance the view from these rooms and to allow for higher, shaped ceilings in the rooms below.

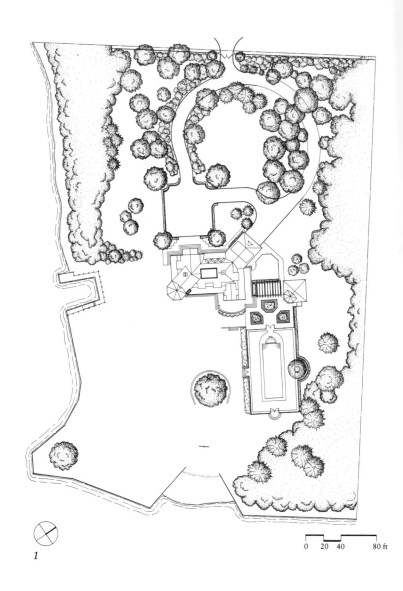

1

0   20   40   80 ft

2

3

4

48

NORTHWEST ELEVATION

SOUTHEAST ELEVATION

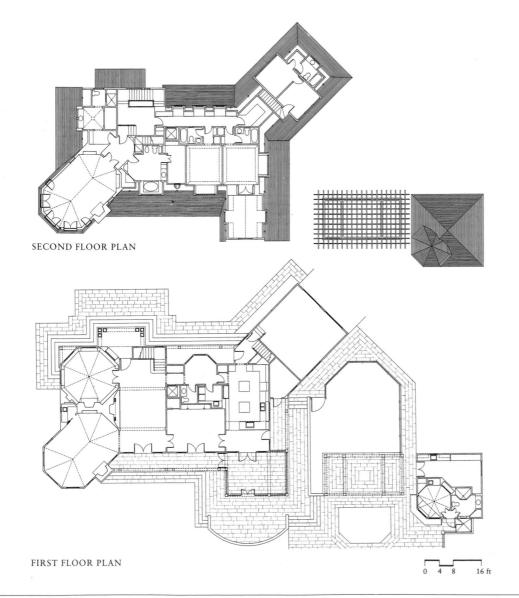

SECOND FLOOR PLAN

FIRST FLOOR PLAN

0 4 8   16 ft

6

7

8

Residence at Calf Creek

Water Mill, New York
1984–87

50 Located along a tributary of Mecox Bay, this house combines picturesque massing and familiar vernacular elements such as a gambrel roof, dormer windows, and projecting bays with more formal classical elements including a stylobate, Tuscan columns, and full entablatures.

Entry is through a vaulted porch that leads into a double-height stair hall. The plan is organized so that the more enclosed service areas are placed along the entrance facade, allowing the principal living rooms to be situated facing the view. Columns and shingled corner piers supporting the paired gambrels of the second floor on the water elevation resolve the asymmetry of the ground-floor plan while providing a large covered porch off the dining room.

Rising at the southwest corner of the house is a tower, much in the manner of a shingled lighthouse. In its base is an octagonal study indirectly lit through an oculus, while at the second floor a winding stair from a bedroom leads up to a playroom with a commanding view of the bay and the ocean beyond.

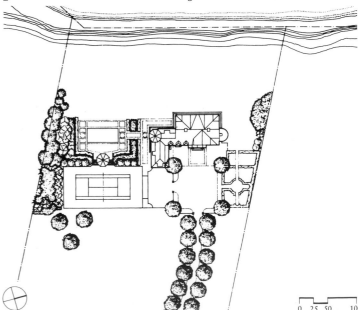

1

2

3

4

5

6

7

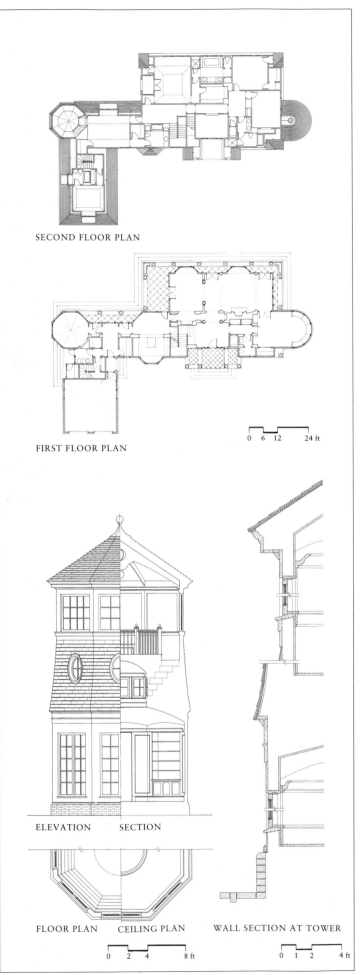

SECOND FLOOR PLAN

FIRST FLOOR PLAN

0 6 12   24 ft

ELEVATION   SECTION

FLOOR PLAN   CEILING PLAN   WALL SECTION AT TOWER

0 2 4   8 ft   0 1 2   4 ft

9

10

11

14

15

16

Frankfurt Jewish Memorial Competition

Frankfurt, Germany
1987

58 The call to create a series of memorials adjacent to the Judischer Friedhof of Frankfurt was one of the most challenging imaginable, given the site's complex history and the social, cultural, and political issues it represents. This proposal consists of individual memorials that relate thematically and spatially to one another so that those who regularly pass through the site and those who visit it as a point of pilgrimage will come away with a sense of the complexity of the past and hope for the future. The set of monuments commemorates the vital contributions of the Jews to Frankfurt and seeks to transform the senseless brutality of the Kristallnacht into a positive lesson for all.

Sheltered in a glass structure reminiscent of the traditional houses that once lined the Jewish Lane, the eternal light, recalling Kristallnacht, will be an optimistic monument to that most enduring yet fragile of human emotions, hope.

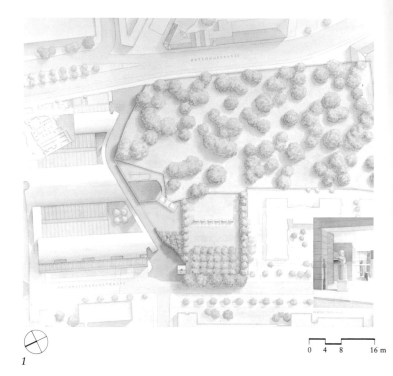

1

0 4 8 16 m

2

Pershing Square Competition

Los Angeles, California
1986

60 This redesign of Pershing Square, the principal but very neglected open space of downtown Los Angeles, recaptures the total available open space for public use. It encourages the kind of activities, both spontaneous and programmed, that once made Pershing Square the civic focus of Los Angeles—a park for all. The square is transformed into a vast outdoor stage, upon which shoppers, office workers, and tourists can act out scenes from the daily drama of urban life. The redesigned square becomes a living room for the city, as well as a microcosm of it; water, trees, and light combine to create a pedestrian-scaled sequence as varied, ever-changing, and kaleidoscopic as that of the automobile-scaled city itself.

Major points of pedestrian access from the surrounding city, as well as from underground parking and future mass transit, are strongly defined: boldly curved, gently sloped ramps sweep up at the corners; columns of water announce mid-block entrances; and welcoming crystal pavilions enhance the sense of arrival from the underground garage. Major paths encourage pedestrians to crisscross the square, forging strong linkages with downtown streets. A water theater lies at the heart of the new Pershing Square, where surging fountains provide constantly changing patterns of light and muffle city sounds.

The crystal pavilions and subsidiary kiosks—with their sleek surfaces of transparent, translucent, and colored glass that sparkle in the sunshine and glow with light at night—are intended to relate to the Persian-inspired forms of the nearby public library and to become unique symbols of Los Angeles.

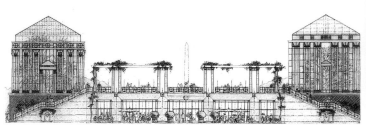

1

0 10 20   40 ft

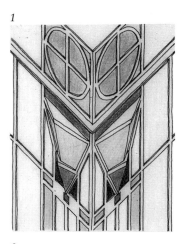

2

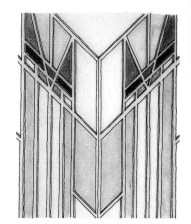

3

4

5

6

The Hamptons

Lexington, Massachusetts
1985–87

62   This development groups six houses along a newly created cul-de-sac in one of Boston's affluent bedroom communities. A consistent vocabulary of shingled walls and roofs, bays, turrets, and covered porches is established; this allows the floor plan, massing, and character of each house to vary considerably without threatening the integrity of the development as a whole.

1. Site plan

HOUSE 1
2. *East elevation*
3. *First floor plan*
4. *View from north*

HOUSE 3
5. *South elevation*
6. *First floor plan*
7. *Entrance facade*
8. *Detail of roof*

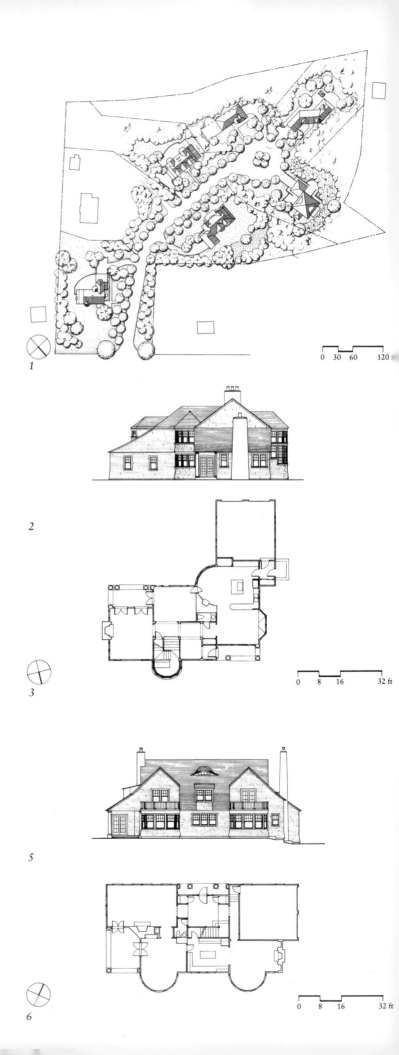

1

0 30 60   120

2

3

0 8 16   32 ft

5

6

0 8 16   32 ft

4

7

8

64

9

10

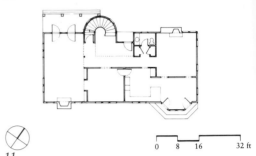

11

12

13

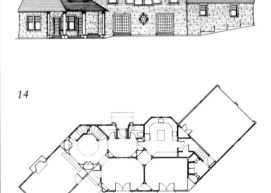

14

15

HOUSE 4
9. View from southeast
10. North elevation
11. First floor plan

HOUSE 5
12. Oblique view of south
    facade
13. Stair hall
14. South elevation
15. First floor plan

0   8   16   32 ft

16

17

18

19

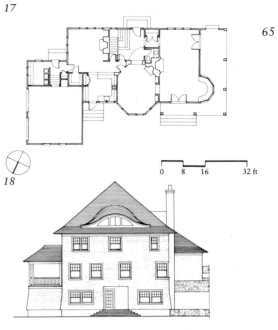

22

23

20

21

HOUSE 7

16. Entrance facade
17. North elevation
18. First floor plan

HOUSE 6

19. View from southeast
20. Detail of north facade
21. Stair hall
22. North elevation
23. First floor plan

0   8   16   32 ft

International Headquarters Mexx International, B.V.

Voorschoten, The Netherlands
1985–87

1. *View across reflecting pool*
2. *Detail of courtyard*
3. *View from southeast*
4. *Existing landmark building, Kempen and Beheer Silver Fabriek*

66   This corporate headquarters combines a renovated 25,000-square-foot, mid-nineteenth-century silverware factory with a new 25,000-square-foot addition. The factory now accommodates executive offices on the ground floor and fashion design studios in what were the second-floor silversmiths' studios, while the addition provides fashion display areas, meeting rooms, a cafeteria, and additional office space. Together the old and new buildings surround three sides of a double-height, south-facing atrium and a reflecting pool. A new employees' restaurant has south- and east-facing glass doors that open to a lawn. The reflecting pool provides animated natural lighting to the ceilings and curved glass walls of the atrium and restaurant. The design strategy attempts to create a retrospective history for the entire building. The structure seems to have grown over time, from the revived baroque classicism of the original facility to the freewheeling shapes of the addition, which evoke the lighthearted and idiosyncratic spirit of 1920s Dutch modernism.

1

2

3

4

68

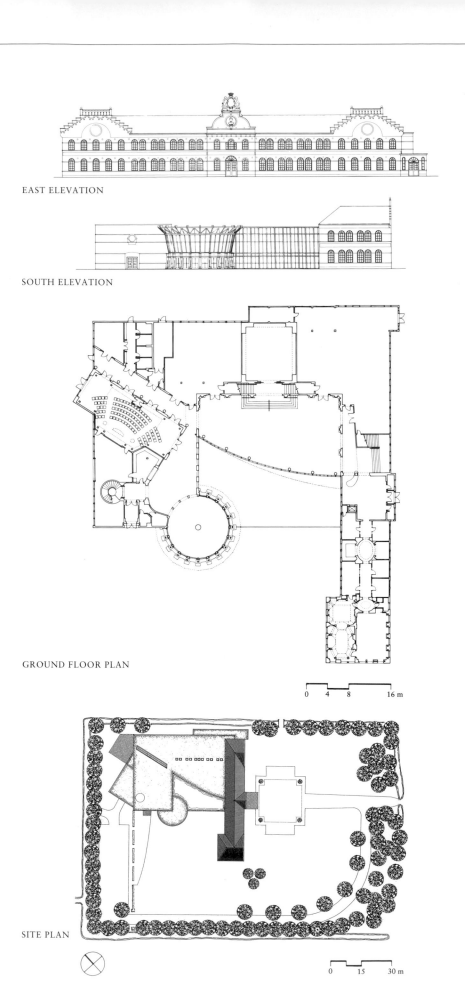

EAST ELEVATION

SOUTH ELEVATION

GROUND FLOOR PLAN

0   4   8   16 m

SITE PLAN

0   15   30 m

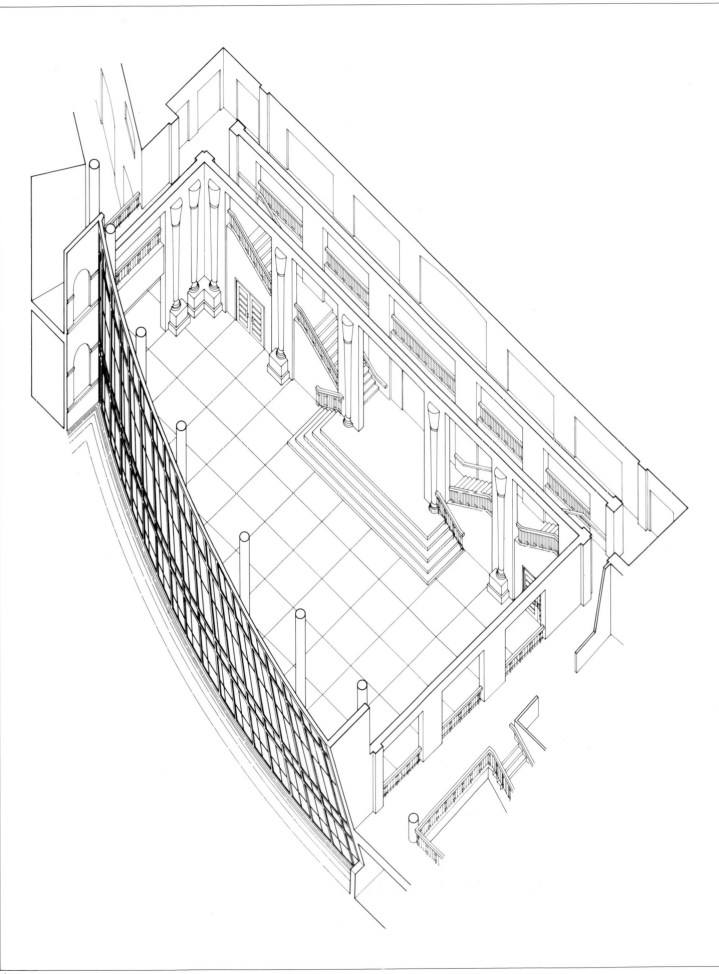

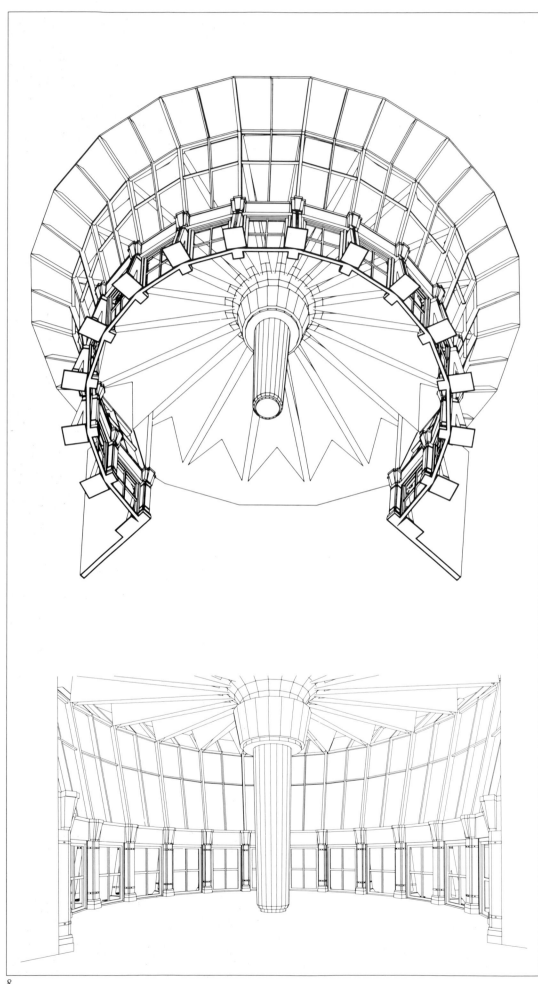

8. Worm's-eye view and
   sectional perspective of
   restaurant
9. Restaurant
10. Executive suite hallway
11. President's office
12. Conference room

9

10

11

12

Mexx, USA, Inc.
Fashion Showroom

New York, New York
1986–87

74   Set in the heart of New York's fashion district, this 10,000-square-foot wholesale showroom combines a feeling of permanence and stability suitable to an established international business with a lighthearted idiosyncracy consistent with the clothes the company sells. The showroom's second-floor location allows visitors to arrive either by elevator or by means of a broad granite and marble stair ascending from the building's lobby. The apse-shaped reception area opens into a sequence of three interconnecting rooms. During the company's seven annual selling seasons these rooms act as a single large gallery where buyers can watch fashion videos while waiting for salesmen. Between seasons large pocket doors can be closed to divide the space into comfortably proportioned meeting rooms.

1

2

3

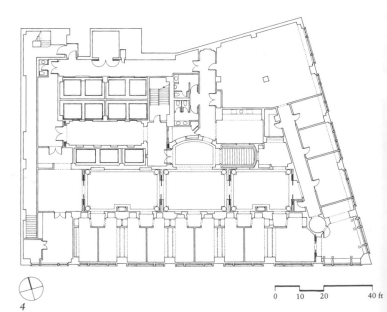

4

0 10 20   40 ft

Mexx Retail Shop

Amsterdam, The Netherlands
1986–87

1. P.C. Hooftstraat elevation
2. Longitudinal section
3. Lower mezzanine floor plan
4. Entry and upper floor plan
5. Street facade

76 Located on Amsterdam's most fashionable shopping street, this 10,000-square-foot shop represents the first venture into retailing for a young and rapidly growing international fashion company. The shopfront is a proscenium arch that opens to the drama within, where not only the merchandise but also the sales help and customers are on stage. Inside, a composition layered from front to back recalls the sets in a theater, and the lighting carries out the dramatic theme with a chiaroscuro quality that accents individual items of clothing rather than bathing the entire space in a uniform light.

The architectural forms are both young and aggressive, in keeping with the company's image. They reinterpret and pay homage to the ebullient if idiosyncratic Amsterdam School architecture of the 1920s. Unlike the brick and wood aesthetic of that work, however, the finishes here are hard and "cool" (glass, brushed stainless steel, and terrazzo) and the colors have been kept to neutral tones to show off the clothes to best effect.

1

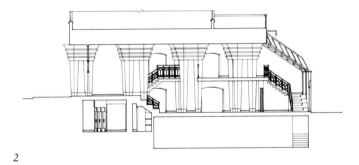

2

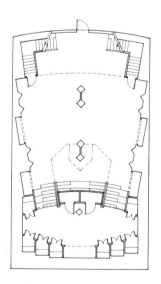

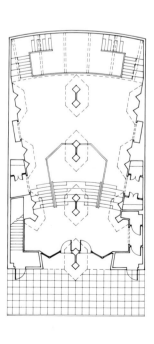

3

0 2 4   8 m

4

78

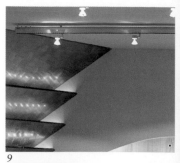

9

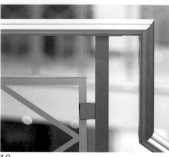

10

6. *Entrance*
7. *Streetscape*
8. *Detail of skylight*
9. *Detail of lighting at column*
10. *Detail of stair handrail*
11. *View toward entrance from lower mezzanine*

6

7

8

Residence

Winnetka, Illinois
1987

80   This house, which was to occupy a corner lot in one of the more established suburbs of Chicago's North Shore, takes its cues from the area's architecture, and specifically from David Adler's Kuppenheimer house, built on the adjacent property. The principal living functions are centralized within a symmetrical, white-painted brick pavilion, from which secondary functions extend in wings. The primary ell, containing bedrooms and a family living room, is disposed perpendicular to the main pavilion, which contains formal entertaining rooms; together they define a sunken courtyard opening off the lower-level indoor pool.

1

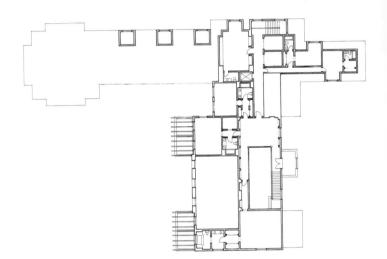

2

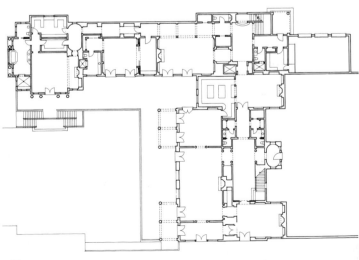

3

0 8 16   32 f

4

5

Akademie der Wissenschaften Competition

Berlin, Germany
1987

82 The design for the new Academy of Science in Berlin was prepared as part of an invited competition. The task was not simply to restore the physical and conceptual integrity of the former Italian Embassy. It was also to challenge that integrity in order to express the new program and, more important, to comment on the extraordinary political changes that have taken place since the embassy was completed in 1943–44. To do this, the architects turned to materials (glass and metal) and forms (dynamic abstract shapes) that symbolize the ideal of science as a process of renewal and defy the static monumentality of Friedrich Hetzelt's somewhat pompous design.

The most prominent new element, the glass pavilion placed before the main facade, leads to a 241-seat auditorium on the lower level. The design preserves the existing circulation pattern, including the original entrance foyer and grand staircase, and introduces a new series of staircases along the wing's inner wall. On the piano nobile the Festsaal is meticulously restored, as are five of the six conference rooms intended for scientific workshops. The corridors and lounges serving these meeting rooms open to the courtyard through the existing windows and a new "break room" housed in an undulating glass bay. At the end of the wing is the new cafeteria, set within a sleekly tapered glass pavilion. A new terrace overlooking the courtyard adjoins the cafeteria. The second floor contains offices for six scientific experts, the president, the secretary general, and administrative staff. At the end of the wing is the glazed library, which contains a concrete study room. A staircase leads to stackrooms and a gallery level. The third floor contains apartments and a lounge for visiting scientists.

The design philosophy for this project is cogently expressed in the courtyard. The fragmentary pergola, damaged during the war, is placed in the context of an exuberantly reconfigured outdoor room that epitomizes the challenge: to "humanize" a building, and to make the new resonate with optimism.

1

2

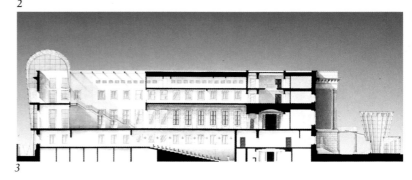

3

1. *West elevation*
2. *Section looking east*
3. *Section looking west*
4. *Axonometric*
5. *First floor plan*
6. *Second floor plan*

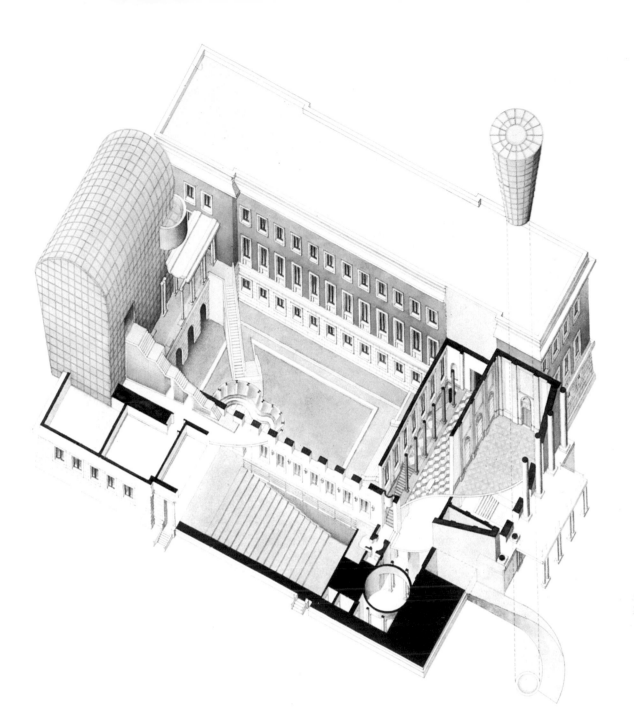

4

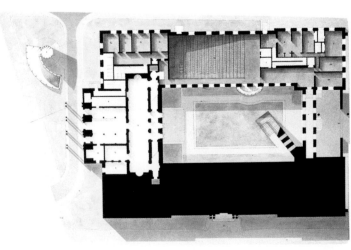

5

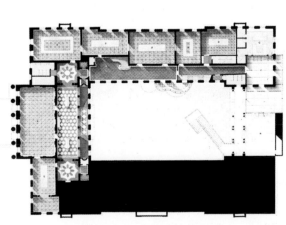

6

84

7

9

10

11

7. *Aerial view of model*
8. *Model from east*
9-11. *Existing conditions*
12. *Model view of courtyard*

8

42nd Street Theaters

New York, New York
1987

1. *Model view looking west on 42nd Street*
2. *Street level plan*
3. *Section*
4. *Perspective of north side of 42nd Street*

86   The reuse of four existing theaters on 42nd Street between Times Square and Eighth Avenue is the subject of a feasibility study sponsored by the New York State Urban Development Corporation. The contiguous theaters—the Selwyn, the Lyric, the Times Square, and the Apollo—represent four very different houses in terms of architectural character, staging potential, and seating capacity. While the general goal of the study was to encourage the return of all four theaters—some of which have been in use as cinemas since the 1930s—to live or media-oriented performance, it also included a proposal for the incorporation of retail and theater-oriented commercial space in and around the theater buildings. This would allow the performance aspect of the entertainment district to be reinforced by appropriately related uses.

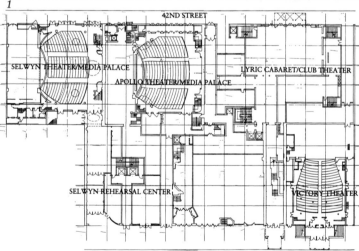

1

2

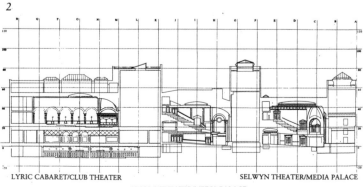

3

0 20 40   80 ft

Residence

Hewlett Harbor, New York
1984–88

88   This house addresses two very different contexts: in front, the gently landscaped terrain of a golf course across the street; in back, a navigable channel that opens through the tidal marshes to Hewlett Bay.

The entry court, a precisely formed exterior room, is bounded by brick walls on two sides and, on the third, by the facade, which takes its cues from Sir John Soane's Pitzhanger Manor and from the Ashmolean Museum by C. R. Cockerell.

The unorthodox six-bay composition of the facade, from which the center column has been omitted, is intensified by the void frieze of the central entablature, the entry-porch roof that spills out from it, and the front door below. Beyond the facade, the Ionic order is used to create a series of rooms where the richly developed scale and detail of classicism are used to articulate the spatial interplay of a modern house. The principal rooms open, through French doors, to a terrace that wraps around the west side of the house, creating a plinth and extending the rooms toward the water.

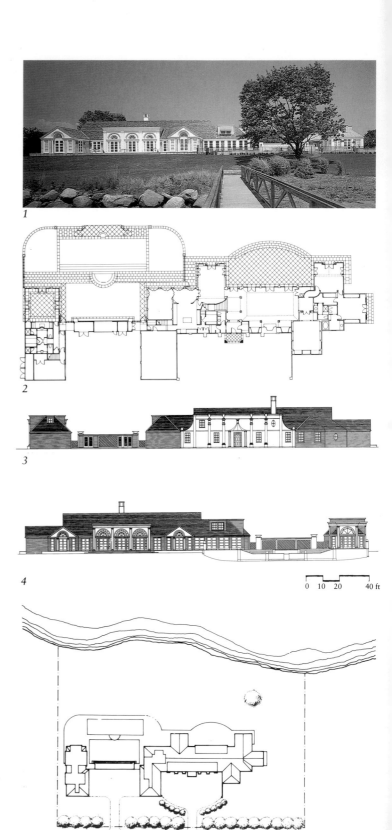

1

2

3

0 10 20   40 ft

4

0   25   50   100 ft

5

7. Living room
8. Staircase
9. Balcony detail
10. Bar
11. Dining room
12. View from entrance hall into living room

7

8

9

10

11

South Pointe Court Competition

Miami Beach, Florida
1988

92 Designed for a limited competition to determine the future of a key two-block site in a Miami Beach neighborhood on the verge of gentrification, this project consists of 210 apartment units ranging in size from studios to three bedrooms. The apartments are located mostly in small four-story buildings that line the periphery of the site, leaving the center for a secure open space. The overall complex is broken up into various villalike units that relate to the scale of the surrounding neighborhood while creating a more intimate, houselike ambience for the residents.

The buildings are arranged along a north-south axis separated from each other by fifty-foot-wide planted courts. As a result, the smaller facades of the buildings face the side streets and the larger facades face the boulevards, an arrangement that not only takes advantage of the prevailing southeast breezes but also shades the side courts from the hottest late-afternoon sun.

1

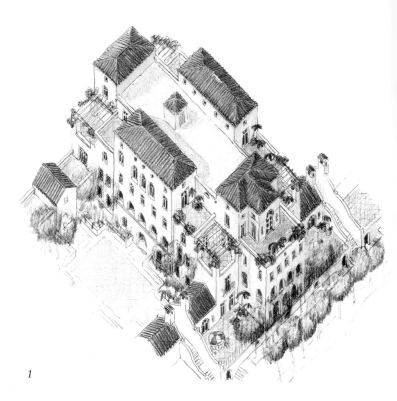

2

3

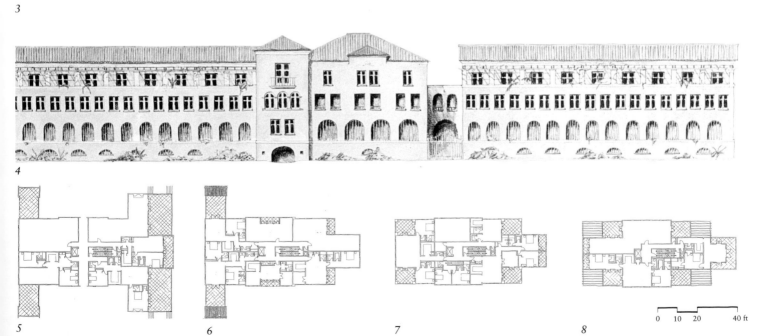

4

5

6

7

8

0 10 20   40 ft

Tegeler Hafen

Berlin, Germany
1985–89

94

This urban villa is one component in the reconstruction of Tegel, a suburb of Berlin ravaged by the war and haphazard postwar planning. The master plan, prepared by Moore, Ruble, Yudell in 1980, calls for the creation of three distinct areas for housing, leisure, and culture. Within the housing district, a five-story serpentine range of row houses provides the background for six freestanding urban villas, each designed by a different architect working within a strict set of design guidelines established by the master plan architects and by the German building code.

In an effort to break with the stark impersonality of most contemporary German social housing, this design recalls the multifamily housing of the fin de siècle, the so-called "urban villas" of Dahlem—one of Berlin's notable suburbs—as well as the cool classicism of Bruno Paul, the distinguished residential architect with whom Mies van der Rohe apprenticed. Traditional gambreled metal roofs, wrought-iron railings, and stucco walls with ceramic tile decoration are composed in symmetrical elevations. In plan, the three-story villa arranges two one-bedroom and four two-bedroom units around a shared daylit stair. All units have a double or triple exposure and all have an outdoor terrace or balcony. The unit plans maintain a balance between the desire for a light, open plan and the need for privacy. Parking and individual storage lockers are located beneath the villa.

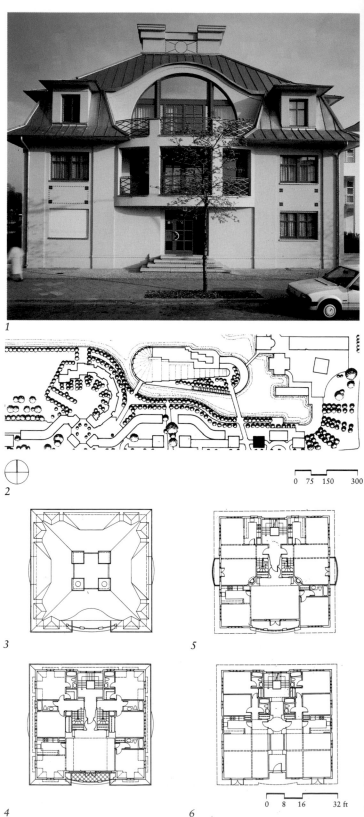

1

2

3

5

4

6

0 75 150   300 ft

0 8 16   32 ft

95

7

8

9

10

Harborview

Baltimore, Maryland
1988

96 Harborview was proposed for a forty-two-acre waterfront site that was once home to shipbuilders. It includes 1,500 residential units, 200,000 square feet of commercial space, and a 666-boat marina.

Despite the high density and tall buildings, the judicious use of setbacks and shaped plans helps to reduce the scale of the complex so that it appears to be made up of clusters of smaller buildings. In addition, small-scale elements have been provided at the bases of the taller buildings to continue the intimate scale of the town-house buildings characteristic of the adjacent upland areas. All the buildings have been given a distinctly houselike quality, with balconies, loggias, pergolas, private gardens, dormer windows, and pitched roofs. Window sizes and spacings are modulated to break down the scale of the facades and to reflect the variety within.

Stylistically, this proposal reflects Baltimore's heritage of classical architecture, a heritage exemplified by the works of Benjamin Henry Latrobe and Robert Cary Long. The complex also takes into consideration the lessons offered by successful large-scale apartment-house complexes built in the 1920s, in particular New York's River House (Bottomley, Wagner & White, 1931).

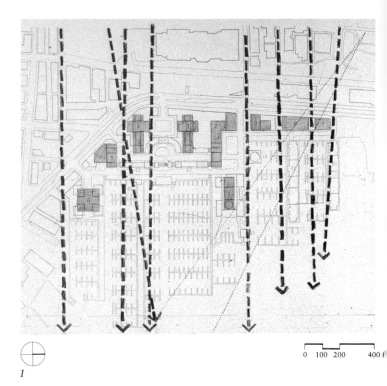

1

0 100 200   400 f

2

3

4

The Shops at Somerset Square

Glastonbury, Connecticut
1986–88

98 Situated in a suburb of Hartford, the Shops at Somerset Square form the heart of a complex of office buildings, housing, and a 300-room hotel.

The design provides a town square for a town that never had one. The new square is surrounded by one-and-a-half-story buildings, the diagonal corners of which serve to reinforce the sense of enclosure. In the square's center a two-story restaurant pavilion glows like a lantern at night, providing a focus. Cars arriving in the square further activate the space, while broad sidewalks allow for comfortable strolling.

The linearity of the retail buildings is punctuated by two-story pavilions that enliven the buildings' silhouette. Similarly composed display pavilions break up the blank walls of the rear elevation and welcome passing motorists. Simple finishes and materials are carefully detailed to articulate a classically inspired composition. Masonry unit walls, finished with the pattern and texture of brick, are painted white; pitched roofs are covered with synthetic slate and crowned by terne-plated ridge caps.

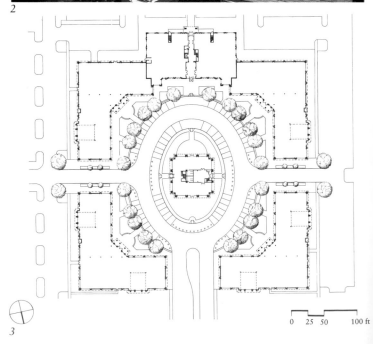

1

2

0   25   50   100 ft

3

4

5

6

California Lifeguard Tower

1988

100   As part of an exhibition at the Kirsten Kiser Gallery in Los Angeles, thirteen architectural firms were invited to reexamine and redefine the lifeguard tower as a building type. From the tall white chairs of the East Coast to the elaborate roofed and decked structures of the West Coast, the standard design has changed little since its inception.

The firm's design of two seated colossi draws inspiration from the ancient past—the great Temple Abu-Simbel in Egypt and the Colossus at Rhodes, one of the Great Wonders of the Ancient World—while simultaneously parodying the narcissistic beach culture of Southern California with monumentalized Ken and Barbie statues.

1

Kathryn & Shelby Cullom Davis Hall, International House

New York, New York
1987–89

102 As part of the firm's ongoing series of renovations to International House, a not-for-profit institution in Morningside Heights in New York City, the 800-seat auditorium has been restored and re-equipped.

Antiquated lighting, rigging, and sound systems have been replaced, seating has been refurbished in the balcony, and modern air-conditioning has been installed. The classical detailing of the original plasterwork, which had been subjected to sixty years of poor maintenance and water damage, was restored to its original condition. An elaborate decorative painting scheme has been executed, utilizing Dutch metal and polychrome glazes in ceiling medallions, ribs, frieze, and proscenium moldings.

1

2

3

4

5

6

7

0   5   10   20 ft

First Government House Competition

Sydney, Australia
1988

104 The program called for two new buildings: a commemorative facility to memorialize the site of Australia's First Government House and, in so doing, to celebrate Australia's early history and complex heritage; and a forty-seven-story office tower designed to go beyond its commercial function and help represent the site on the Sydney skyline. The two buildings, vastly different in program and scale, are juxtaposed in a way that allows each building to be true to its own identity while acknowledging and respecting the other's and the overall context.

The commemorative facility, located in the southeast corner of the site, takes its orientation not from the city's grid but from that of First Government House itself. Designed as a distinct entity, it combines traditional monumentality with an optimistic orientation, expressed by the high-tech rooftop shade canopy. The tower's faceted form was adopted to minimize its impact on views from the existing Legal and General Building, to relate to the intersecting street grids that define the site, and to enhance its reading as an iconic landmark. Above the six-story base of the tower, similar in bulk to the adjacent Education Building, two-story corner pavilions help facilitate the transition from the nineteenth-century scale of the city to that of our own time.

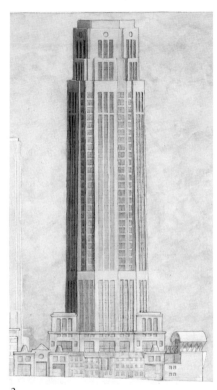

1   2

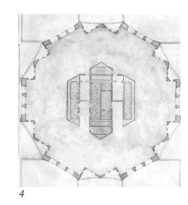

3

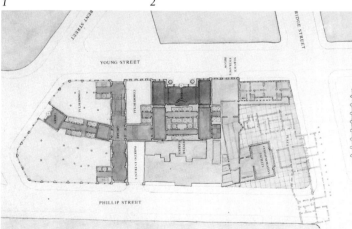

4

Residence

Pottersville, New Jersey
1985–89

106 The house nestles into the brow of a low ridge that crowns a rolling meadow in rural New Jersey. A long, low silhouette is presented to the south, but to the north, where the site falls off, a rubble-clad basement story is exposed, offering a more impressive mass. The composition is elemental, with two juxtaposed gambrel-roofed masses pinned by an octagonal stair tower, echoing neighboring barns and silos.

Entrance to the house is from the west, on the short elevation, so that rooms are open to the best views offered to the north and south. The front hall doubles as a stage used for musical concerts sponsored by the family. The audience for such events sits in the large living room. The east end of the house is reserved for informal family life. Casual meals and television viewing take place in the family room, which at one end is a plant-filled solarium that doubles as an office. At the extreme eastern end of the house is a screened porch that restates the low-pitched, templelike entry portico and overlooks the swimming pool and a broad expanse of meadow.

1

2

3

4

5

108

NORTH ELEVATION

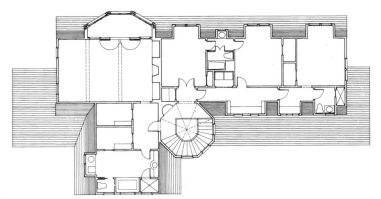

SECOND FLOOR PLAN

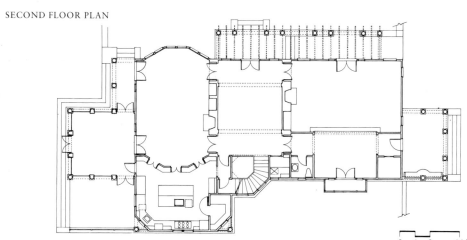

FIRST FLOOR PLAN

0   4   8   16 ft

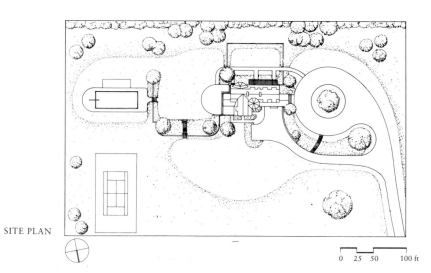

SITE PLAN

0   25   50   100 ft

7

8

9

Grand Harbor

Vero Beach, Florida
1986–89

112 Set on the Indian River, Grand Harbor is a resort community built around two golf courses and a marina. The original components of this design were Harbor Center, including 90,000 square feet of retail space with 116 residential units above, and Wood Duck Island, a separate complex incorporating sixty-seven town houses and three clubhouses—one each for golf, tennis, and swimming. The town houses were completed, but Harbor Center and the clubhouses remain unbuilt.

Harbor Center incorporates shops, restaurants, and a market to serve not only the Grand Harbor community but also residents in the greater Vero Beach area as well as tourists. Stucco walls, clay tile roofs, shutters, arcades, and small courts evoke the Mediterranean quality of Addison Mizner's Worth Avenue. Apartments above the retail space promote a planning ideal: a mixed-use village center rather than a shopping mall.

The clubs and town houses of Wood Duck Island were designed to work together as a cohesive urban unit with a hierarchy of streets and paths, landscaped walls, and intimate courts. The clubs were grouped to create a formal plaza, providing the gateway from which a grand boulevard leads to the villas, which, in turn, are arranged around small courtyards.

Each grouping of houses is composed of four closely related types interlocked in an orderly fashion that also creates a relaxed and picturesque feeling. Stucco walls, clay tile roofs, and shutters evoke farm groupings in Andalusia, Spain, but are here given a more distinctly classical feeling.

0   500   1000

1

2

3

4

5

7

8

9

10

11

Kol Israel Synagogue

Brooklyn, New York
1985–89

This synagogue for a growing
congregation occupies a corner site in an
established residential neighborhood. To
complement the watery Mediterranean
quality of the surrounding houses, a
vocabulary of red brick and stone walls
sheltered by a red tile roof was adopted.

Stringent setback and height limitations
led to an unusual arrangement whereby
the entire site was excavated to 10'6"
below grade. This created the largest
possible area for the light-filled main
sanctuary, which rises up past the entry
level and balconies to achieve a height of
thirty-four feet.

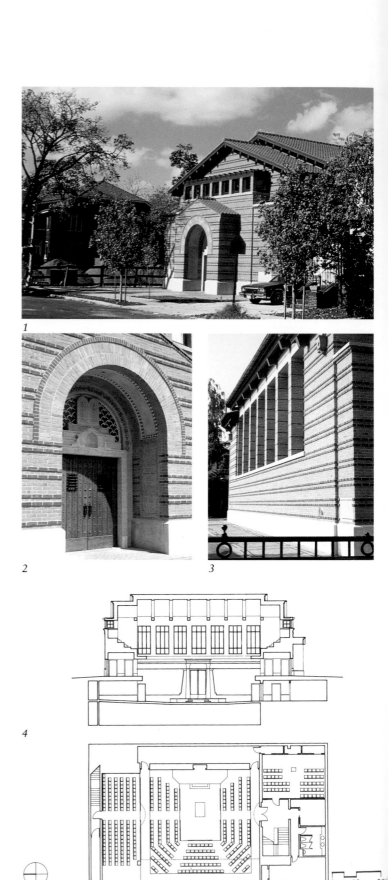

1

2

3

4

5

6

7

8

1. *View from Avenue K*
2. *Entrance portal*
3. *West facade along Bedford Avenue*
4. *Longitudinal section*
5. *Congregation level plan*
6. *Entrance facade*
7. *Tile pattern study*
8. *Sectional detail*

Residence on Russian Hill

San Francisco, California
1985–89

120   This extensive reconstruction and expansion of one of the oldest houses on Russian Hill consists of two significant compositional devices: a picturesque tower located asymmetrically at the northwest corner, where it forms a dramatic entry; and a straight run of stairs that cuts across the building to lead visitors to the principal living rooms located on the top floor, affording spectacular views of the San Francisco Bay area. Although the austere shingled idiom of the original house is retained in this reconstruction, the new tower and the detailing of the entrance porch begin to suggest the intricate play of planes and volumes that occurs on the interior.

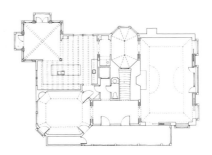

1

2

3

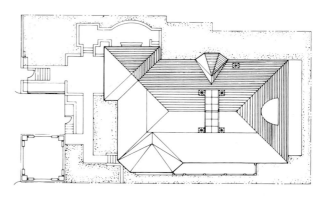

4

5

6

7

8. View from bottom of
   Russian Hill
9-12. Details of entrance
13. Living room
14. View of stair to master
    bedroom
15. Principal stair

8

9

10

11

12

13

14

15

Residence at Conyers Farm

Greenwich, Connecticut
1986–89

124 Against a part-butterfly plan configuration derived from McKim, Mead and White's Cowdin and Misses Appleton houses, this residence juxtaposes exterior massing and details that evoke the architecture of the English Arts and Crafts and American Craftsman movements.

The main floor parti straightforwardly opens the library, living room, and dining room off a generous entry/stair hall. Shifts in the plan off from the orthogonal axes, meanwhile, lend interest to the sequence of spaces. The interior detailing continues the aesthetic already developed on the exterior, particularly in the double-height timber-framed living room, where elements such as a massive rubble-stone fireplace, clerestory dormers, and a monumental oriel window help to further articulate the design intentions.

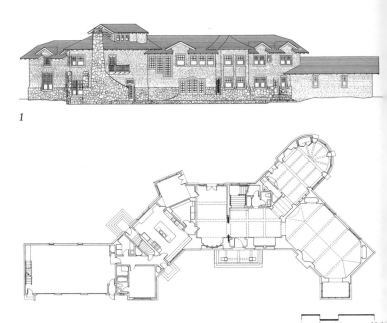

1

2

0 8 16 32 f

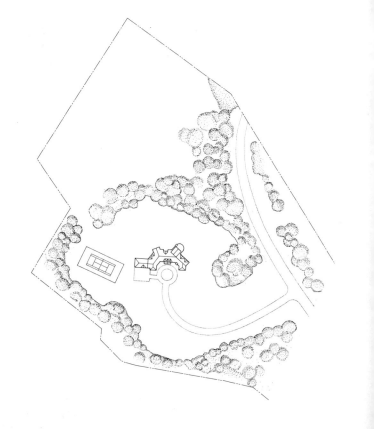

3

0 80 160 320 f

Residence

Elberon, New Jersey
1985–89

126   This seaside villa is composed of simple stucco volumes capped with red tile roofs. The main house, only one room thick and L-shaped in plan, is set behind a wall that traverses the site to provide privacy on the entrance side while admitting western light through a cloistered garden.

The house opens to the ocean across a limestone terrace with broad steps cascading down to a rolling lawn and the beach beyond. Off to one side a second set of terraces steps down to a cabana and a tiered pool that creates the illusion of fresh water flowing into the sea.

The Mediterranean quality of the house, a stylistic reference that is in keeping with its neighborhood, is deliberately casual. The detailing is restrained: on the exterior, dark red tile roofs, terra-cotta cornices, Tuscan red painted windows; inside, polished mahogany doors set in rough plaster walls, oak beamed ceilings, and stone floors.

1

2

3

4

128

SECTION FACING NORTH

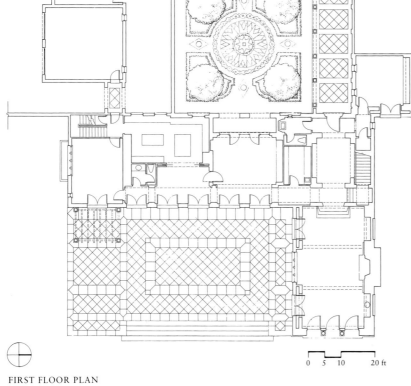

FIRST FLOOR PLAN

0 5 10   20 ft

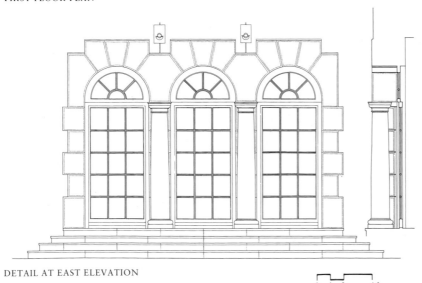

DETAIL AT EAST ELEVATION

0 1 2   4 ft

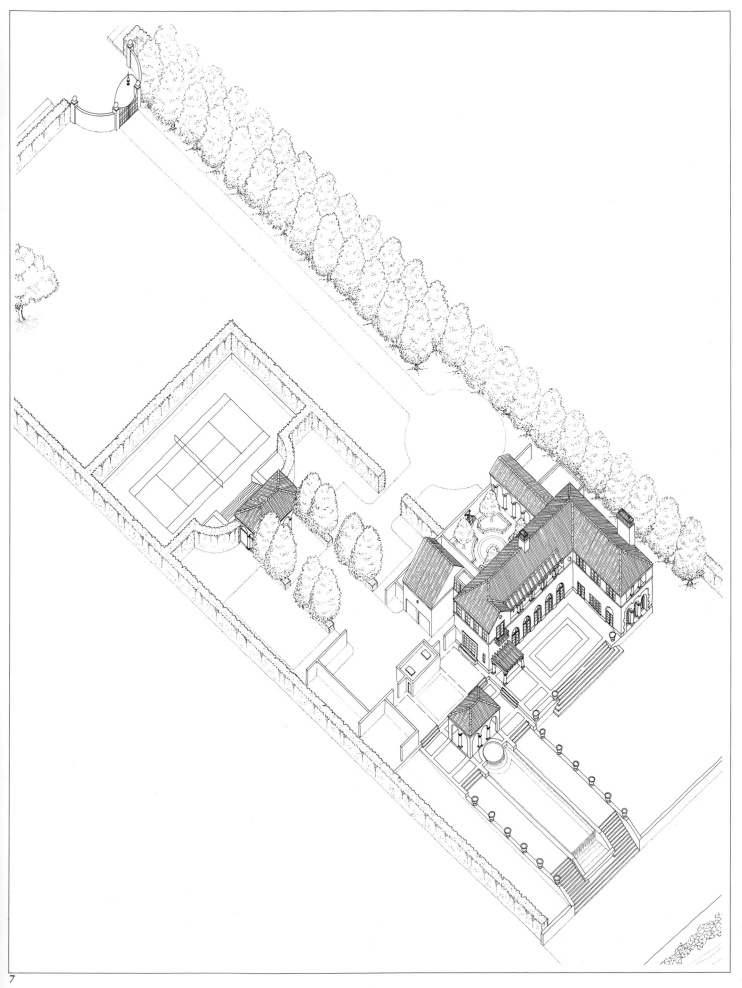

8

9

10

11

131

12

13

14

City Hall Complex
Competition

Orlando, Florida
1989

132 Prepared for a limited competition, this design groups a ten-story city hall and municipal office building and a pair of twenty-two-story speculative office buildings around a plaza intended to function as a traditional town square.

In contrast to the bland, flat-roofed high-rises and self-important "signature" towers that characterize Orlando's downtown skyline, the new city hall complex was conceived as a series of carefully sculpted masses. The octagonal hipped-roof form of the city hall building was designed to shelter a four-story room with ceiling murals depicting historically important moments in Orlando's development. The junction for a number of arcades that connect the municipal offices to the surrounding mixed-use development, this room functions as a public parlor for city organizations whose activities and celebrations could easily open out to the plaza in good weather.

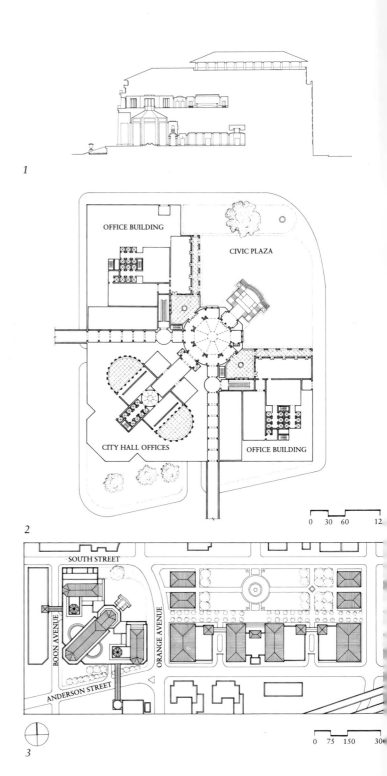

1

OFFICE BUILDING

CIVIC PLAZA

CITY HALL OFFICES

OFFICE BUILDING

0 30 60   12

2

SOUTH STREET

BOON AVENUE

ORANGE AVENUE

ANDERSON STREET

0 75 150   30

3

133

4

5

6

House at Wilderness Point

Fishers Island, New York
1986–89

134   This house is an expression of both the architect's and the clients' desire to emulate and continue the rich tradition of Shingle Style architecture that characterizes the growth of Fishers Island during its greatest development in the early part of the century. Riding the crest of a ridge on a fieldstone base, the house is only one room deep in order to take advantage of the breezes and to allow for the water views on both sides. These considerations led to the linear arrangement, with the continuous gable of the main mass punctuated by pavilions and elements such as a tower and a gazebo.

1

2

3

4

EAST ELEVATION

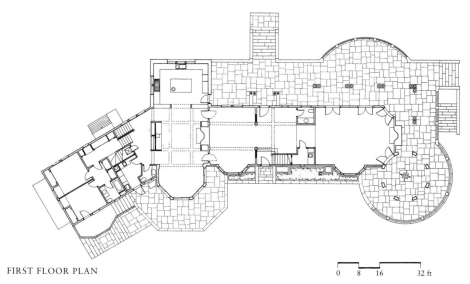

FIRST FLOOR PLAN

0   8   16   32 ft

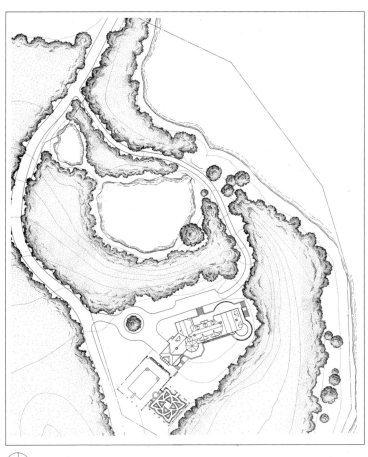

SITE PLAN

0   30   60   120 ft

7

8

9

Master Plan and Fine Arts Studio IV, Fine Arts Village, University of California, Irvine

Irvine, California
1986–89

140 The master plan is intended to guide the expansion of the university's fine arts complex through the year 2010. The ideas developed in the master plan for the Fine Arts Village were later carried further in a plan that combined fine arts and humanities into one village. The master plan not only deals with issues of program and growth but also calls for a new architectural vocabulary using red tile roofs, arcades, and naturally ventilated spaces in an effort to counterbalance the aesthetic and environmental problems posed by the first buildings of the Fine Arts Village.

Studio IV, an art studio and a facility for dance and drama rehearsal, represents the first phase of the long-term master plan to be realized. It transforms what was the back of the Fine Arts Village into a new front door, facing both a major campus access road to the north and the recently completed University Events Center. The building also creates a new south-facing amphitheater-like plaza, which serves as a gathering area or outdoor "commons" for all art students. Using light-frame and industrial building techniques, the new structure provides a maximum of open loft space within a limited budget. A design studio and slide library at the lower level open directly to the lawn. Above are two large rehearsal halls: one for the dance program; the other, a black box theater, for drama students.

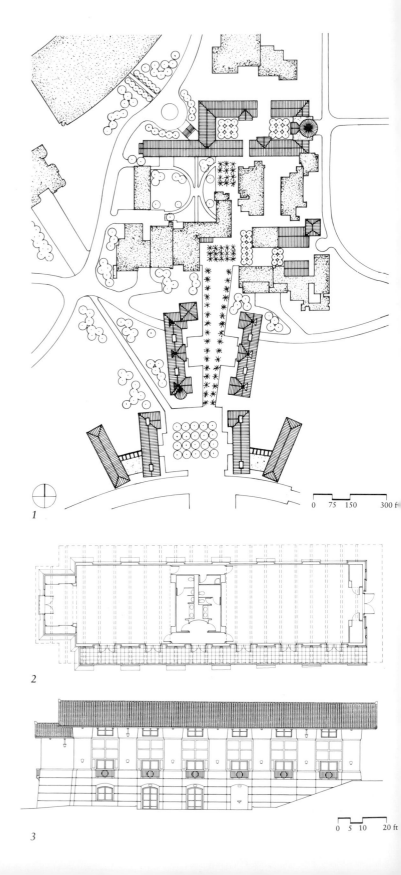

1

0 75 150 300 ft

2

3

0 5 10 20 ft

4

5

6. West facade
7. East facade
8. Detail of southwest corner
9. View from northwest

6

7

8

Centro Cultural de Belem Competition

Lisbon, Portugal
1988

144 The firm's entry to the limited competition for the proposed Belem Cultural Center incorporates a large conventional hall, a congress hall for the European Common Market, a museum for the city of Lisbon, hotels, shops, and underground parking. While most of the construction was to be new, some historical architecture is incorporated in the complex; the design seeks to capture and continue the essential features of Lisbon's traditional waterfront urbanism—bold ramparts, intimate scale, oases of greenery.

The 100,000-square-foot exhibition building at the eastern edge of the site consists of a vast, unified hall at grade level and three glazed pavilions above. Stairs lead visitors to the terraces set between the pavilions and onto the aerial walkways that traverse the roadway below.

The entrance towers, whose glazed conical roofs echo a Portuguese architectural tradition in a new material, border the terrace, which constitutes a formal entrance court to the conference center, museum, and concert and lecture hall.

Beyond these buildings, a central plaza leads past a shady bosque to two inns, retail spaces, and a variety of pedestrian and vehicular passageways. In sharp contrast to the formal court to the east, the plaza is multi-leveled and bowl-like, forming a stage for the theater of urban life.

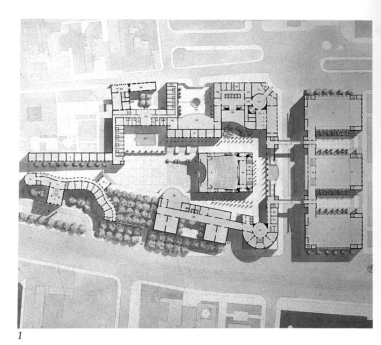

1

2

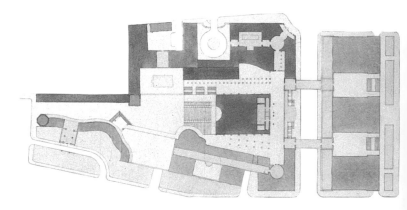

3

0 10 20   40

4

5

Casting Center
Walt Disney World

Lake Buena Vista, Florida
1987–89

1. *View from west*
2. *Entrance*
3, 4. *Exterior details*
5. *Night view of entrance*

146 The Casting Center faces Interstate 4 but is entered from Buena Vista Drive within Walt Disney World proper. The sole representation of the Disney company along the interstate, the building is intended not only to house personnel functions but also to convey the company spirit to prospective employees. It accommodates the central hiring facility as well as offices for the Employee Relations Division and the Labor Relations Department. The design of the 360-by-80-foot, 61,000-square-foot building—organized as two blocklike abutments and a bridge spanning a marsh—represents a journey from unemployment to employment. The southern end of the bridge houses the entrance rotunda, while the northern end contains the building's principal room, the General Employment Lobby, located on the second floor.

Inside and out, the casting building abounds in imagery culled from Disney's movies and theme parks: campanile-like skylights, turrets, finials, futuristic airfoil shapes, and elaborately tiled surfaces, as well as Mickey Mouse water scuppers. Visitors enter under the airfoil canopy, open bronze doors with handles modeled on a character from *Alice in Wonderland,* and move through a processional sequence of spaces that starts in an oval rotunda adorned with twelve gilt statues of Disney's most illustrious characters illuminated from above by a glazed campanile. Continuing along a 150-foot-long skylit ramp lined with trompe-l'oeil panels that offer highly interpretive views of Disney World as well as the immediate roadside context, the job seeker is introduced to the heart of the building without violating the privacy of workers who occupy the two floors of offices. The ramp is not only a way to effectively handle the large crowds of job applicants but also a surrogate for the visitor's experience in the Disney parks, where ramps are used to channel crowds and heighten the sense of expectation for individual attractions. The trip up the ramp culminates in the General Employment Lobby, located under the second campanile.

1

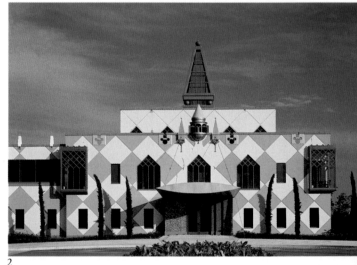

2

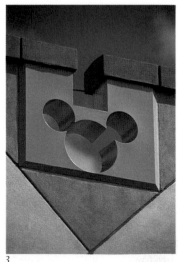

3

4

6. *Section through entrance lobby and site plan*
7. *Elevation, section, and plans*
8. *View from southeast*

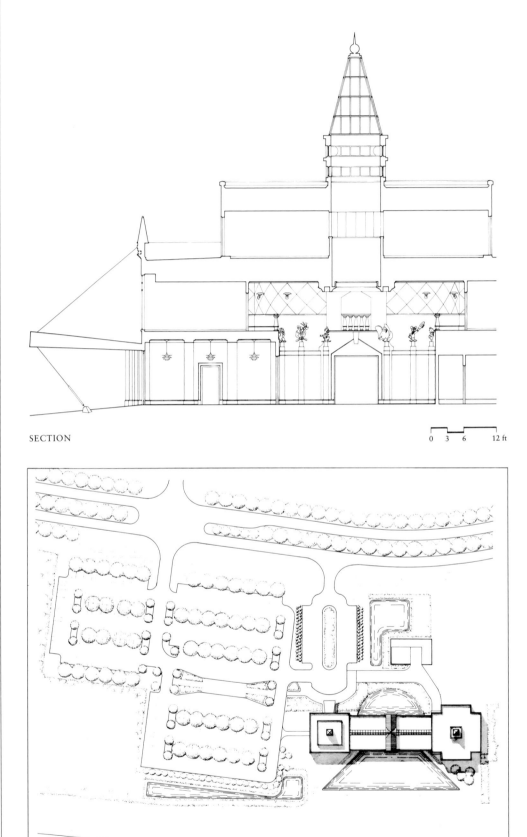

SECTION

0   3   6   12 ft

SITE PLAN

0   30   60   120 ft

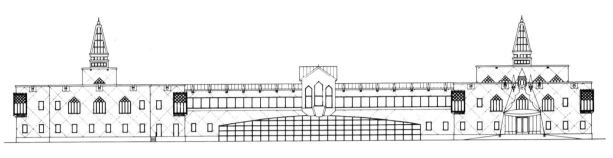

WEST ELEVATION

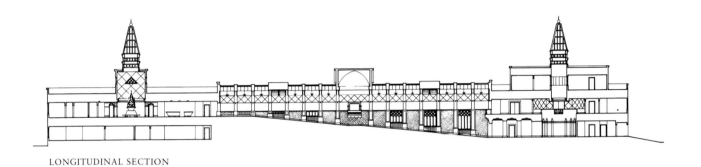

LONGITUDINAL SECTION

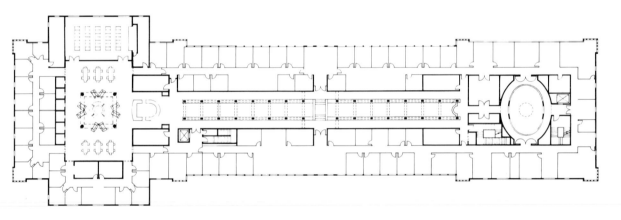

SECOND FLOOR PLAN

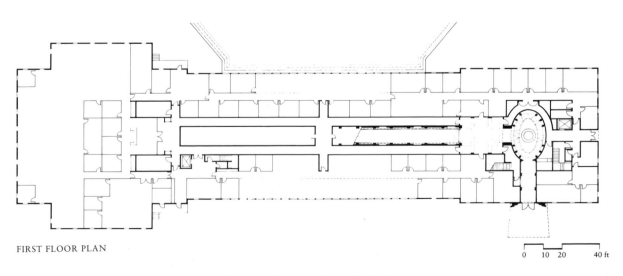

FIRST FLOOR PLAN

0 10 20   40 ft

Independence Public Library

153

10

11

12

13

14

15, 16

Offices for Capital Research Company

New York, New York
1987–89

1. *Typical office*
2. *Floor plan*
3. *Reception lobby*
4-6. *Furniture studies*

156   This design for the 22,000-square-foot New York offices of an international asset-management firm reflects its location in Rockefeller Center's International Building and suggests that the suite of rooms has been in place since the building's opening in 1935. The lobby, boardroom, and gallery spaces for the client's significant art collection constitute one unit. With panels of anigre and bubinga woods and limestone floors, they carry forward the suave modern classicism of Rockefeller Center's architecture.

Where day-to-day operations are conducted, the vocabulary is pared down to create a more open, informal atmosphere. Partners' offices have built-in work stations containing personal computers, Quotron machines, a coat closet, and generous shelving, as well as lighting. At the core, a large library, open to view through a continuous band of glazing, provides a literal and symbolic focus.

1

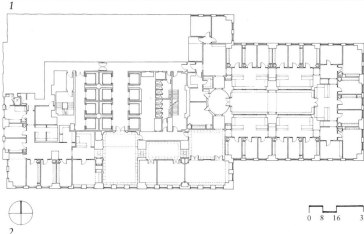

2

3

4

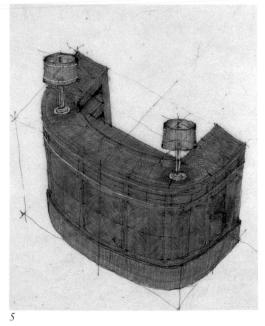

5

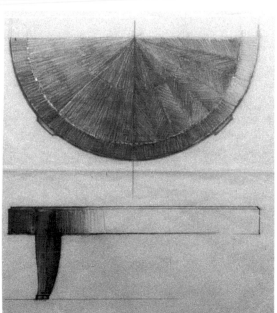

6

7

9

8

10

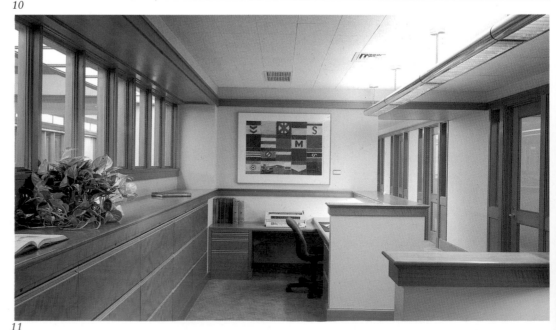

11

159

12

13

14

Bancho House

Tokyo, Japan
1988–89

1. *Section through penthouse apartment*
2. *Penthouse floor plan*
3. *Location plan*
4. *View of penthouse from ambassadorial garden*

160 Bancho House, a five-story office building surmounted by a two-story residential penthouse, overlooks the British Embassy. From its top floors there are sweeping views of the Imperial Palace gardens and the skyline of the Marunouchi district, Tokyo's main business center.

Sheathed in flamed Absolute Black granite and honed Atlantic Green granite, stainless-steel-finished aluminum, and gray-tinted glass, Bancho House synthesizes modern elements and traditional classicism as a gesture both to the architecture of the seventy-year-old British Embassy and to the client's preference for traditional Western architecture. The principal rooms of the penthouse open out onto a rooftop terrace, which is framed by pergolas at either end, sheltering it from neighbors and emphasizing the dramatic view to the southeast.

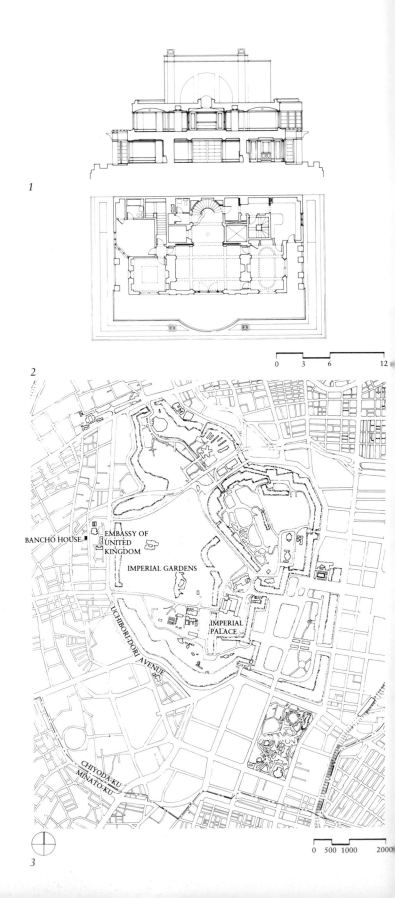

162

7

8

5

6

Morton Street Ventilation Building Competition

New York, New York
1989

164   This proposal is for two forty-five-foot-tall towers, connected underground, and an electrical transformer house to serve the PATH train system in an environmentally sensitive setting facing the Hudson River. The towers provide emergency smoke ventilation and passenger egress. They are a principal feature of the new esplanade that will eventually extend between Piers 40 and 45 and be bounded on the east by a riverfront boulevard, the successor to the Westway proposal of the 1980s. This project has been under scrutiny by community groups and the West Side Waterfront Panel, who are studying both the size and architectural character of the towers and the future use and character of the waterfront.

Our proposal, prepared for a two-way competition, was directed toward tailoring these buildings to the fixed dimensional requirements of the machinery and ventilation chambers they contain while creating contextually sympathetic, appropriately scaled, and well-configured architectural and landscape forms. The classical vocabulary of the design, which includes brick and stone, relates the new towers to the character of the immediate upland neighborhood, particularly the Greek Revival houses along Morton Street and contiguous blocks. The towers' bold scale and simple details fit in well with the neighboring late-nineteenth- and early-twentieth-century warehouses, which are also classical in design.

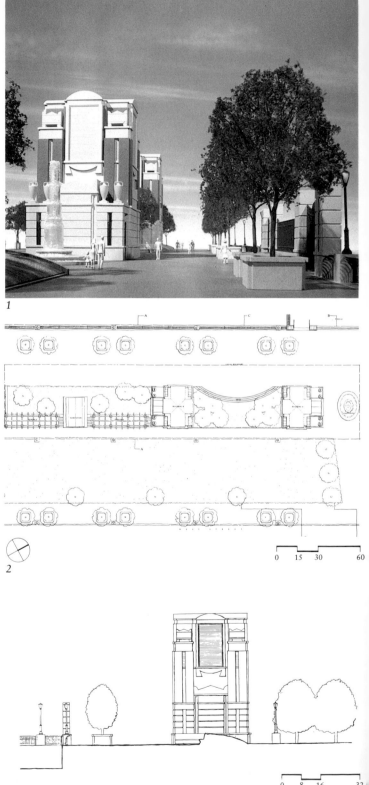

1

2

0   15   30   60

3

0   8   16   32

1. *Model view along esplanade*
2. *Site plan*
3. *Section at esplanade*
4. *View from Hudson River*
5. *Perspective looking west*

4

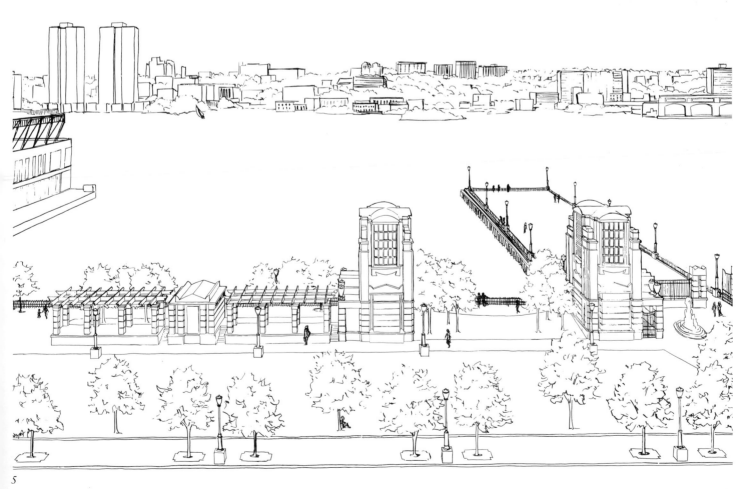

5

The Country Club and Houses for the Villages at Rocky Fork

New Albany, Ohio
1989

1. Clubhouse, entrance floor plan
2. Site plan
3. Clubhouse, west elevation
4. Aerial perspective of village looking southeast
5. Perspective of club and villas looking west

166 A master plan for the Villages at Rocky Fork, a suburb of 500 houses in Columbus, Ohio, is organized around a golf course and country club that would be the central features of the new community. Prototypical house designs of different areas and lot sizes were prepared for the "villages"—arranged in circles, squares, and boulevards—whose character derives from the landscaped spaces they enclose.

A first phase of approximately eighty-five houses was developed for a village surrounding the new golf club, embracing a parklike practice fairway adjacent to the golf course. A mix of small, medium, and large houses incorporating walled gardens and arranged in small groups or enclaves engages the landscape along classical vistas and sightlines to distant objects.

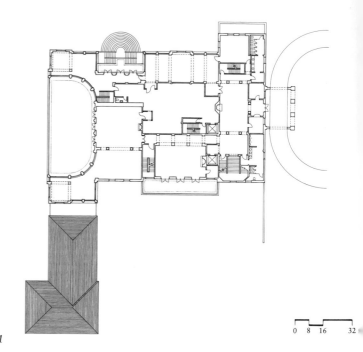

1

0 8 16 32

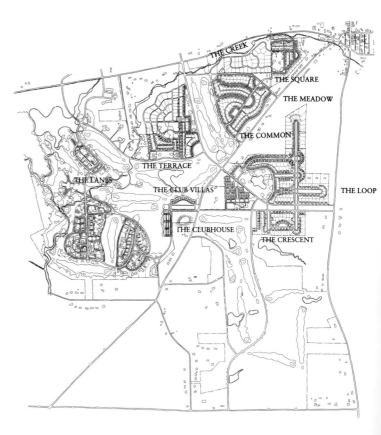

0 500 1000 2000

2

3

4

5

The Terrace, Village I

168

The Loop, Village IV

The Square, Village II

The Common, Village III

The Meadow, Village III

The Crescent, Village V

Addition to a Cottage

East Hampton, New York
1989–91

170   Purchased as a modest cottage of uncertain but not antique age, this house has been gradually changed over a period of ten years. In the renovations, the classical language of architecture has been used in varying degrees of literalness to organize the volumes and give them scale. In the original renovation this language was used in a very abstract way: inside, dadoes and cornices were defined by the most minimal of moldings, and columns were two-dimensional cutouts. In the most recent addition of a master-bedroom suite, the work of two early-nineteenth-century classicists has been the inspiration. The thick-walled architecture of the suite accommodates books and artifacts in a spatially complex way, as in the library at Sir John Soane's house in London. Outside the room is a classical pavilion that confronts the garden with a facade inspired by the dining room of Jefferson's Monticello.

Also planned is a new living room contained within a shingled tower, which, paired with an existing wing, will bracket the pergola and create a balanced facade facing the hedge garden.

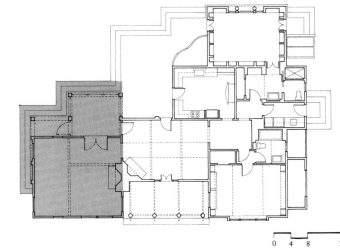

1

2

3

4

5

6

Skyview

Aspen, Colorado
1987–90

172   This house is set on the steep slopes of
Red Mountain, facing Aspen Village and
the renowned ski slopes above it. It is
organized along a straight run of stairs
that leads down from the entrance and
past various elements of the plan arranged
in half-level increments, culminating at a
two-story piano-curved wall of glass that
directs the eye to the valley floor below.
At the lowermost landing a cross-axis,
organized as gently terraced platforms,
connects the dining room, the double-
height living room, and the billiards room
to the swimming-pool terrace beyond.

The living areas are situated along the
south face to take full advantage of light
and view, while service areas are bermed
into the hill. The plan is cranked to
minimize the structure's apparent length.
Drawing inspiration from the clustered
forms of traditional hill towns, the
massing is articulated into small elements,
creating the impression of a main
community house and individual
children's houses to the side. A simple
palette of tawny beige stucco walls set
atop a native sandstone base, metal
roofing, and natural wood trim allows the
house to blend into its site.

1

2

1. *View from northeast*
2. *Entrance*
3. *View from southeast*
4. *Site plan*

3

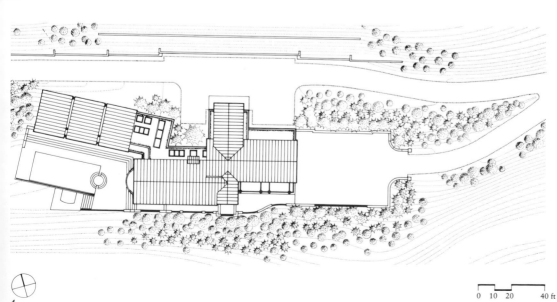

4

0 10 20 40 ft

175

6

7

8

9

10

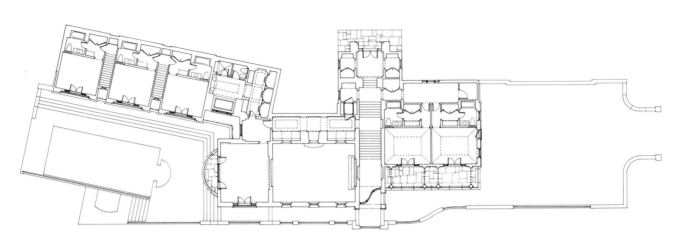

SECOND FLOOR PLAN

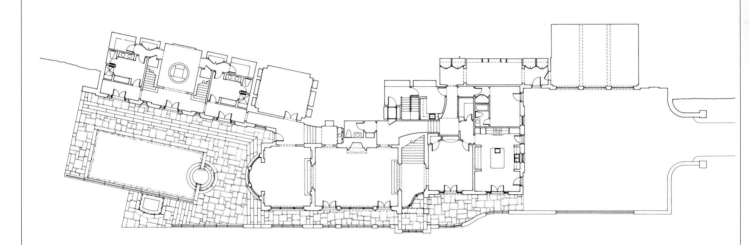

FIRST FLOOR PLAN

NORTH ELEVATION

0   5   10   20 ft

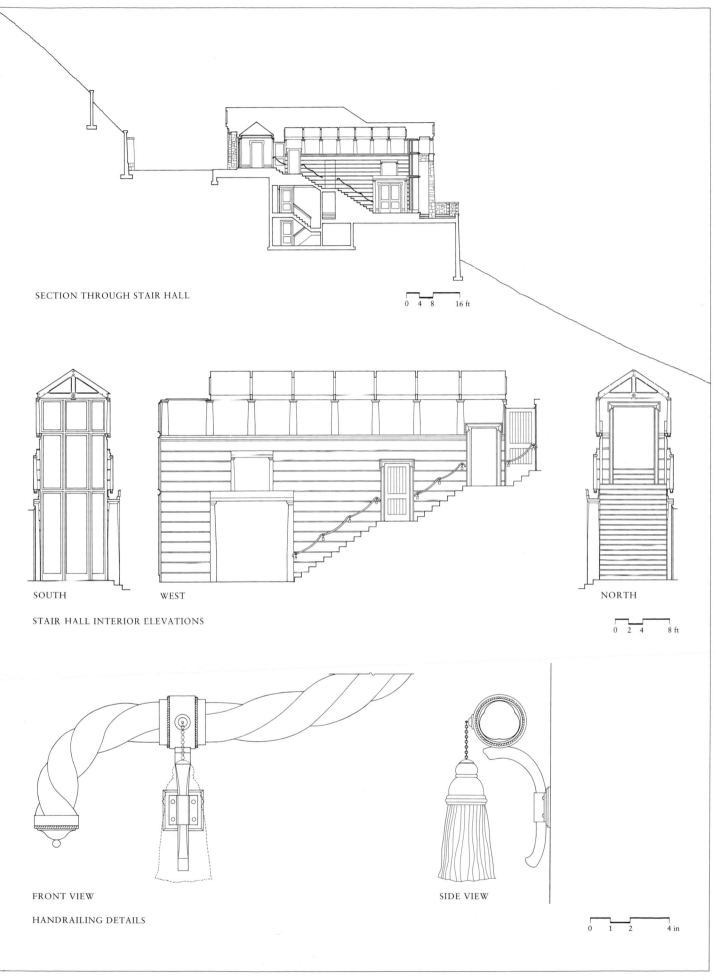

SECTION THROUGH STAIR HALL

0 4 8   16 ft

SOUTH   WEST   NORTH

STAIR HALL INTERIOR ELEVATIONS

0 2 4   8 ft

FRONT VIEW   SIDE VIEW

HANDRAILING DETAILS

0 1 2   4 in

178

13

14

15

16

Police Building

Pasadena, California
1987–90

180   The Police Building is the first major addition to the Pasadena Civic Center to be undertaken in twenty years. Located at the intersection of Walnut Street and Garfield Avenue, it occupies a subordinate position in relation to the landmark City Hall (John Bakewell, Jr. & Arthur Brown, Jr., 1925–27), Public Library (Myron Hunt & H. C. Chambers, 1927), and Civic Auditorium (Bergstrom, Bennett & Haskell, 1932).

The building's focal point is a tower capped by an open-air loggia, recalling the colossal open-air dome of City Hall. Located asymmetrically, this tower is visually buttressed by a two-story arcaded porch supporting scrolled volutes. The porch, which helps enclose a courtyard and is related in scale to the adjacent Southern California Gas Company building (architect unknown, 1924), leads to a three-story entrance lobby. Although the building is one in which security is paramount, the appearance of an armed fortress is carefully avoided—the Police Building expresses civic grandeur while maintaining a welcoming public image.

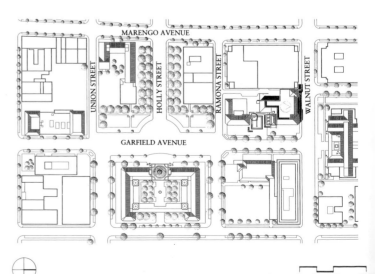

1

2

0   10   20   40

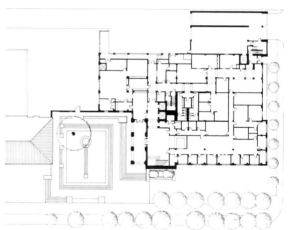

3

0   75   150   300

4

5

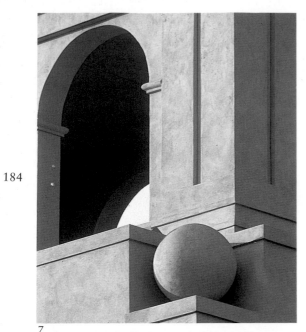

7

8

7, 8. Exterior details
9. Entrance lobby
10. View from second floor
    overlooking City Hall
    dome

Community Services

9

Two Venture Plaza
Irvine Center

Irvine, California
1988–90

1. *View from east*
2. *Site plan*
3. *Approach*

186   This 100,000-square-foot, five-story office building is located in an office park at the confluence of two of Southern California's busiest freeways. Within the office park it occupies a pivotal corner site, but access to the building is possible only through an interior cul-de-sac. The building is sited at an angle to the corner to heighten its impact and to address the entry drive, which slices diagonally across the square site from the cul-de-sac. Twin parking structures, linked underground, flank the entry drive, helping to reinforce the approach axis leading to the entry court.

A two-story freestanding porch, supported by four truncated obelisks capped by shallow metal urns, marks the entrance. Fifth-floor balconies, appropriate for the mild Southern California climate, together with the broad projecting silver metal visor, provide a strong skyline silhouette.

1

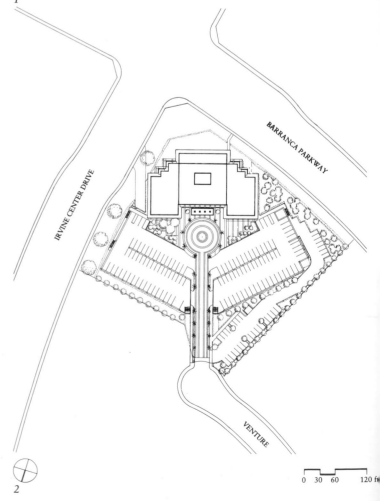

2

0 30 60 120 ft

4. *View from north*
5. *South facade*
6. *Corner detail*
7. *Porte cochere light fixture*
8. *Night view of porte cochere*
9. *Entrance lobby*

4

5

6

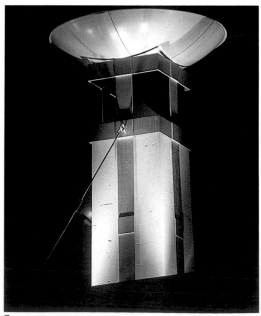

7

Residence

Bloomfield Hills, Michigan
1989–90

1. *Approach to house*
2. *Detail of garden facade*
3. *Southwest corner*
4. *First floor plan*
5. *View from southeast*
6. *View from garden*

192   This red brick Georgian-style house, located in a well-established residential area, is nestled between mature trees at the entrance and a steep slope to the rear that provides a view of a heavily wooded area to the west. The entrance facade yields a double-scale reading: it is quite grand from the street but more comfortable within the forecourt. The garden facade is bolder, exposing more of the central two-story mass of the house and allowing principal rooms maximum exposure to both southern and western light and views.

1

2

3

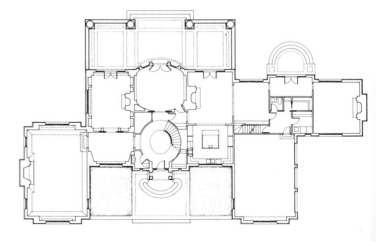

4

0   6   12   24

5

6

Apartment Building, Surfers Paradise

Queensland, Australia
1989

194   This thirty-one-unit luxury apartment tower, restaurant, and marina complex was projected for a site on the Nerang River near the heart of Australia's most popular resort city. Amidst the resort's random urbanism, the site is organized as a series of discrete outdoor rooms. Arriving visitors are taken past a gatehouse, a covered parking garage, and an inner portal, into a large forecourt with a ramp up to the tower's porte cochere and entrance lobby. Beyond the tower forecourt a third portal leads to a restaurant and marina overlooking the river.

Classical principles established in the site planning are carried through to the massing and details of the building: a columnar shaft culminates in a series of setbacks where penthouse apartments enjoy lavish garden terraces.

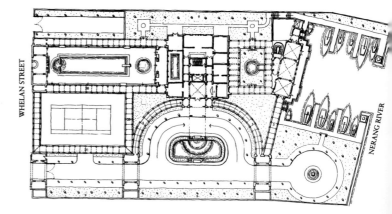

1

2

0 5 10 20

3

4

5

Kiawah Beach Club

Kiawah Island, South Carolina
1989–90

196   The Kiawah Beach Club was intended to provide oceanfront recreational and dining facilities in this island resort as an amenity for homeowners in the immediate area as well as for golfers at the championship oceanside course to the east. As the physical and functional center of the scheme, the dining pavilion provides a filtering buffer between the entry motor court and parking lots to the west and north and the swimming pool and beach areas to the east and south. Flood-zone restrictions dictate that the entire complex be elevated well above grade; as a result, the stairs that mediate the ensuing changes in level become major architectural elements, integral to the plan and massing of the project.

While the pavilion and its outbuildings owe their basic form to such low-country precedents as Mulberry and Drayton Hall, their detailing in cypress and cedar and their reliance on shading devices such as wood blinds and lattice are rather more Caribbean in influence. The intention was also to introduce to Kiawah the canvas-tented private cabana, a feature that was a fixture at mid-Atlantic clubs before the age of air-conditioning. These would line the boardwalks leading out from the club to the ocean.

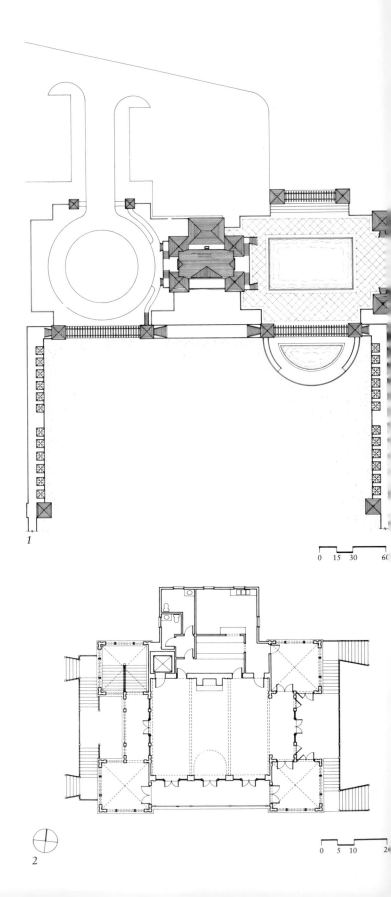

1

0   15   30   60

2

0   5   10   20

1. *Site plan*
2. *First floor plan*
3. *Aerial perspective from south*
4. *Beach elevation*

3

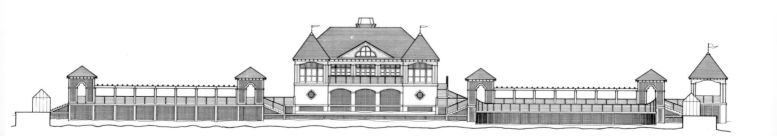

4

```
0    10   20        40 ft
```

"New York: Yesterday, Today, and Tomorrow" Metropolitan Home Showhouse II

New York, New York
1991

198 The 1991 showhouse, to benefit the Design Industries Foundation for AIDS, was in a brownstone town house on East Seventy-ninth Street. This design transformed the front parlor into an idealized representation of the high-style glamour and modern sophistication that, through the medium of 1930s and 1940s films, has become one of the most enduring symbols of Manhattan life.

1

2

Product Design

1

2

3

4

5

6

7

8

9

10

11

12

16

17

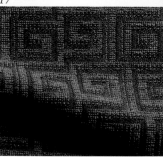

18

13

14

15

BED LINENS FOR
ATELIER MARTEX

12. *Triomphe*
13. *Newport Gardens*
14. *Hyannis*
15. *Pompeii*

TEXTILES FOR HBF

16. *Ferronnerie, Dionysian,
    Volute*
17. *Empire*
18. *Meander*

19. *Owligorical House for
    Parish Art Museum*

Espace Euro Disney

Villiers-sur-Marne, France
1990

204 The firm's responsibility on this project was to create a site plan and a facade for a collection of prefabricated buildings that would provide a small retail outlet, a food concession, a lobby with a model of the future Euro Disneyland, and a theater where the resort will be previewed.

The building has been located on the site so that the primary facade is rotated slightly toward the direction of most of the guest traffic. The parking is kept to the side, while an entry court is created in front of the building, allowing all visitors to approach the building from the same direction—whether they are arriving in a tour bus or walking from the parking lot.

As the French public's initial exposure to a Disney building in the Paris area, this facility needed first and foremost to capture the spirit of this unique enterprise in the same way that a nation's pavilion at a world's fair strives to capture the essence of the country it represents. Here are combined bright colors and kinetic lights, lively shapes and patterns, and familiar iconography.

The hat Mickey Mouse wears as the Sorcerer's Apprentice provides the shape for the tower marking the entrance to the building's primary function—the preview theater—while at the same time alluding to the "Disney magic" to be found in the theater inside. A balcony above the front door contains a Disney character welcoming guests to the center. The entrance to the Disney retail outlet is masked by a small purple facade with a Mickey cutout, while a large yellow wall behind features chase lights on wavy blue lines and separate, randomly illuminated lights on red dots, which together give the effect of confetti.

The food concession to the left of the main building mass is fronted by a billboardlike red wall with silhouettes of iconic Disney characters as they seem to walk to the building entrance. The figure/field colors are reversed as the characters continue to march across the front of the arcade in a manner that suggests a series of film negatives.

1

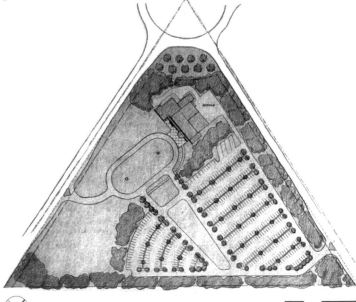

0 25 50 100

2

1. *Detail of entrance*
2. *Site plan*
3. *Night view of entrance facade*
4. *Floor plan*
5. *Section*
6. *Principal facade*

3

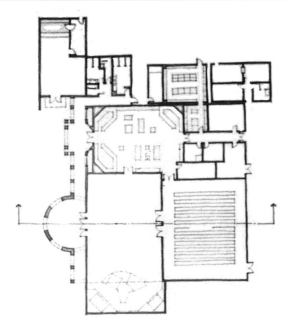

4

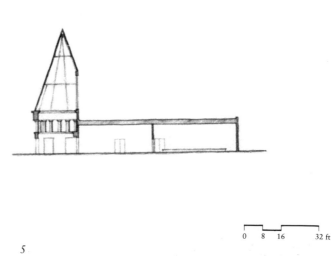

5

0   8   16   32 ft

Washington State Labor and Industries Building Competition

Olympia, Washington
1990

208 This 440,000-square-foot, state-of-the-art facility for the administration of the state labor relations and insurance agencies was designed for a three-way competition. The heavily wooded site is in a suburb of the state capital. Two similar buildings, linked by a central lobby, are oriented to optimize sun exposure and vehicular access. The program of the building is a complex one, involving a hierarchy of public access and security issues, as well as a wide variety of planning and construction requirements.

The building incorporates traditional architectural elements of wall, arch, and cornice in a nontraditional manner. Stone, clear and reflective glass, and weathered and painted metal are combined to create an architectural character that is both rustic and technically progressive, qualities that are in keeping with the natural surroundings and the built context.

The lobby is crossed at three levels by free-span bridges within an arched, glass-walled space that permits an unobstructed view through to the landscaped setting of the project. Public spaces are organized around a courtyard whose central feature is a cascade.

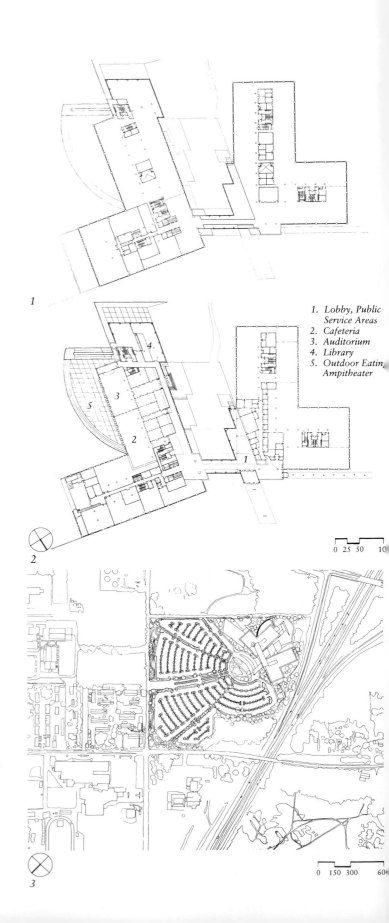

1. Lobby, Public Service Areas
2. Cafeteria
3. Auditorium
4. Library
5. Outdoor Eating Ampitheater

0 25 50 10

0 150 300 60

1. *Second floor plan*
2. *First floor plan*
3. *Site plan*
4. *Perspective from Interstate 5*
5. *Perspective of entrance*

4

5

222 Berkeley Street

Boston, Massachusetts
1986–91

1. *View from Massachusetts State House*
2. *View from Boston Common*
3. *View east along Boylston Street*
4. *View across Charles River and Back Bay*
5. *Elevation, section, and site plan*
6. *Axonometric of lobby and winter garden*
7. *Winter garden*

210

A mixed-use building in Boston's Back Bay combining 520,000 square feet of offices, shops, a winter garden, and a 400-car-capacity underground garage, 222 Berkeley Street is the second phase of a controversial major retail-office complex in one of America's most architecturally elaborate yet fragile urban centers.

The familiar Boston palette of red brick, granite, and limestone has been adapted to a complexly massed office tower, shaped in response to the different urban pressures on each of its sides and resolved in a pavilion-like crown to create a distinctive skyline silhouette that places the building firmly within the American tradition of classical skyscrapers.

The main lobby, reached through a severely classical portico facing Berkeley Street, leads past the office lobby to monumental stairs rising to the second-story winter garden, a top-lit, five-story-high room that functions as light court and public gathering place. A continuous row of shops faces Boylston Street, interrupted at one point by an entrance leading to the north-south mid-block pedestrian arcade. To emphasize the public nature of the arcade and the winter garden it leads to, the Boylston Street entrance is flanked by paired Ionic columns holding urns and features a revolving door housed in a tempietto.

1

2

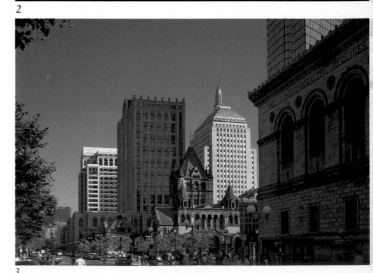

3

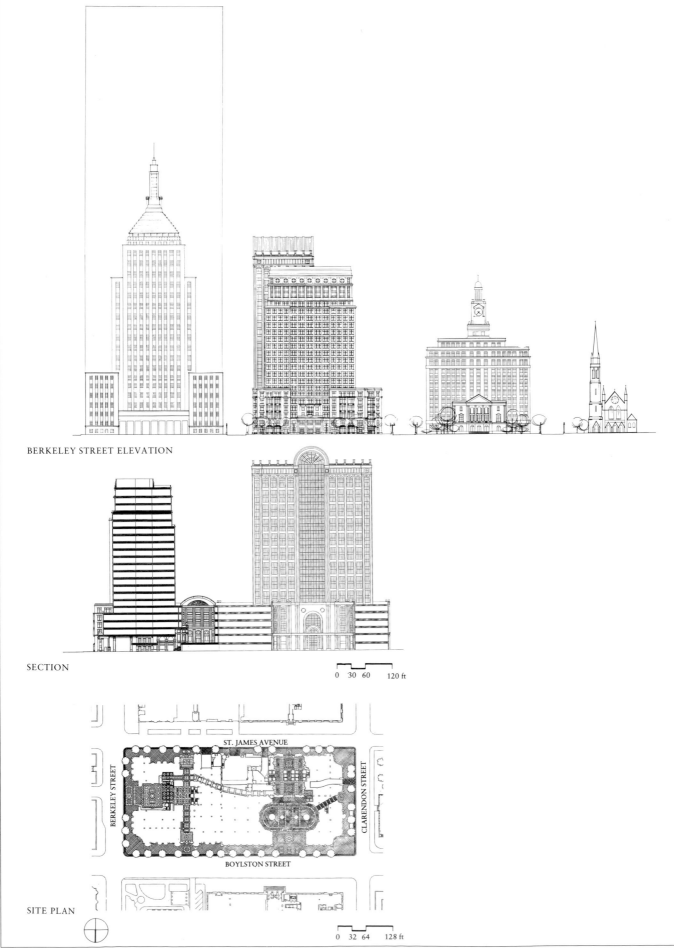

BERKELEY STREET ELEVATION

SECTION

0   30   60   120 ft

ST. JAMES AVENUE

BERKELEY STREET

CLARENDON STREET

BOYLSTON STREET

SITE PLAN

0   32   64   128 ft

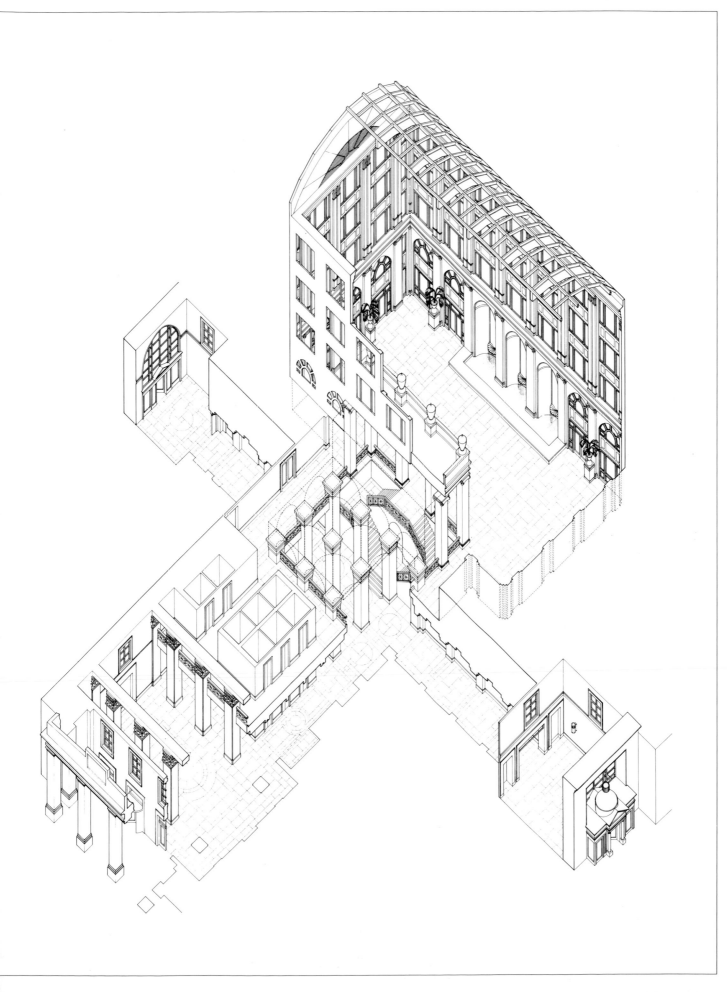

8

10

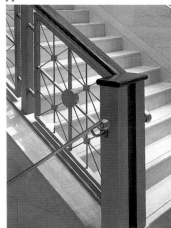

11

9

12

8. Berkeley Street entrance
   lobby
9. Vaulted hall
10-12. Interior details
13. Boylston Street entrance

218

14

16

14. *View across Boston Common*
15. *Berkeley Street facade*
16. *Cornice detail*
17. *View from Copley Square*

15

Cap d'Akiya

Hayama, Japan
1987–

220   The firm's first building designed for Japan, this seaside apartment house is to be built some thirty-five miles south of Tokyo in the Hayama district. Many weekend homes and apartments in the neighborhood take advantage of the hilly Sagami-wan coastline and the distant views of Mount Fuji.

The combination of the program (eleven apartments ranging from 1,400 to 2,700 square feet, including a luxurious penthouse; and a rooftop pool and terrace shared by all residents), the site, local fire-code requirements, and height and sun shadow restrictions contribute to the building's specific sense of place.

However, this building should also be understood as part of a long tradition of interaction between Western and Oriental cultures. The design, evoking feudal Japanese castles such as the Osaka Castle (Toyotomi Hideyoshi, 1583–86), perhaps the most formidable fortress in Japan, also looks to Frank Lloyd Wright's Japanese work, and that of Edwin Lutyens in India, to create a complex layering of form and meaning.

0   12.5   25   50

1

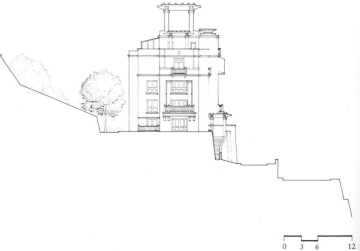

0   3   6   12

2

3

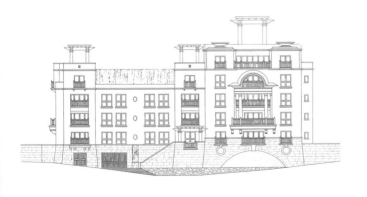

4

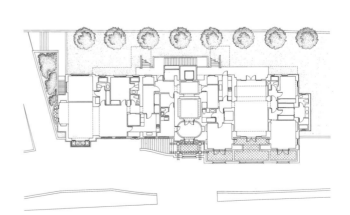

5

Spruce Lodge

Old Snowmass, Colorado
1987–91

222 Set atop a knoll along a creek in a valley of the Rocky Mountains, this log and shingle house combines two characteristic American house types—the Adirondack camp and the Rocky Mountain ranch house—to create a picturesque massing of projecting bays and dormers that complement the rugged surroundings and frame spectacular views.

The free yet carefully articulated plan opens to the landscape through a combination of screened-in, covered, and open porches and balconies off the principal rooms, which extend along the southern facade. Entry is through a porte cochere into a large vestibule that leads to the double-height living room. Framed with heavy timber trusses, dominated by a Colorado sandstone fireplace, and opening to the view through glass doors and tall windows, this room serves as a grand gathering space at the heart of the house. The second floor is separated by the living room into two wings, one for children and guests and one for the master suite.

1. *Southwest elevation*
2. *Site plan*
3. *First floor plan*
4. *Second floor plan*

1

2

0 20 40   80

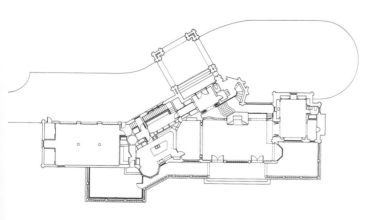

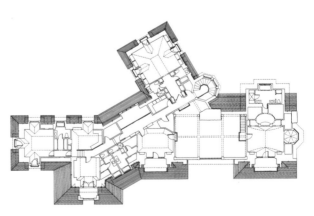

0 10 20   40 ft

3   4

Ohrstrom Library
St. Paul's School

Concord, New Hampshire
1987–91

224   In 1985–86, the office studied ways to add on to the existing Sheldon Library, designed for the school by Ernest Flagg in 1901. The proposal for the addition would have expanded Sheldon to twice its original size while maintaining its inherent spatial and formal qualities.

When the school's trustees decided to build a new library, a prominent site at the center of the villagelike campus was selected. This design for the Ohrstrom Library forms the boundary wall for two quadrangles: to the south it joins a residential group to create an intimate courtyard; to the north it is the edge of a larger space that is both the symbolic and the actual center of the campus, serving as a counterpoint to the school's original chapel (1859) and Henry Vaughan's masterly essay in the Gothic, the Chapel of St. Peter and St. Paul (1888).

While H. H. Richardson's Crane Library, Quincy, Massachusetts (1880–82), inspired the plan and the handling of the red brick and Briar Hill stone used for the exterior, the design was also influenced by the synthesis between traditional form and modern abstraction in the library C. R. Mackintosh designed for the Glasgow School of Art (1907–09). This is apparent in the tall oriel windows, the abstraction of detail, and the mediation between the small scale of the residential buildings and the buttressed structure of the Chapel of St. Peter and St. Paul.

On the inside, the principal point of reference was James Gamble Rogers's School House (1937), until Ohrstrom the last building in St. Paul's School's chain of Gothic-inspired buildings. Ohrstrom Library incorporates the most up-to-date computerized information-retrieval technology into traditional reading rooms and more intimately scaled niches that provide a variety of places for quiet individual or group study within easy reach of the bookstacks. The navelike plan is entered at the crossing that separates the stacks from the specialized reading rooms, the primary one being a two-story-high vaulted room that opens to a view of Lower School Pond.

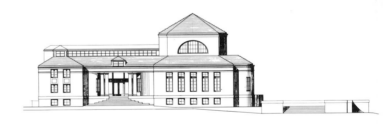

1

2

3

4

5

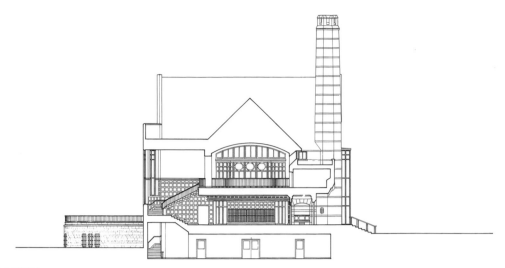

SECTION FACING WEST

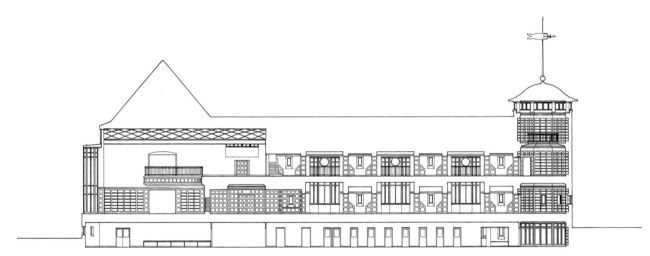

SECTION FACING NORTH

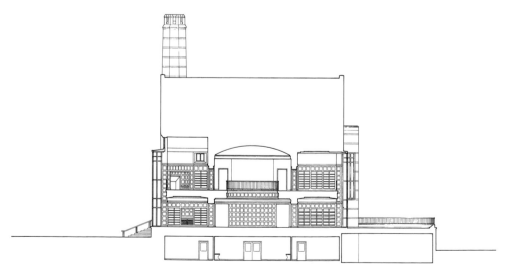

SECTION FACING EAST

0   6 12   24 ft

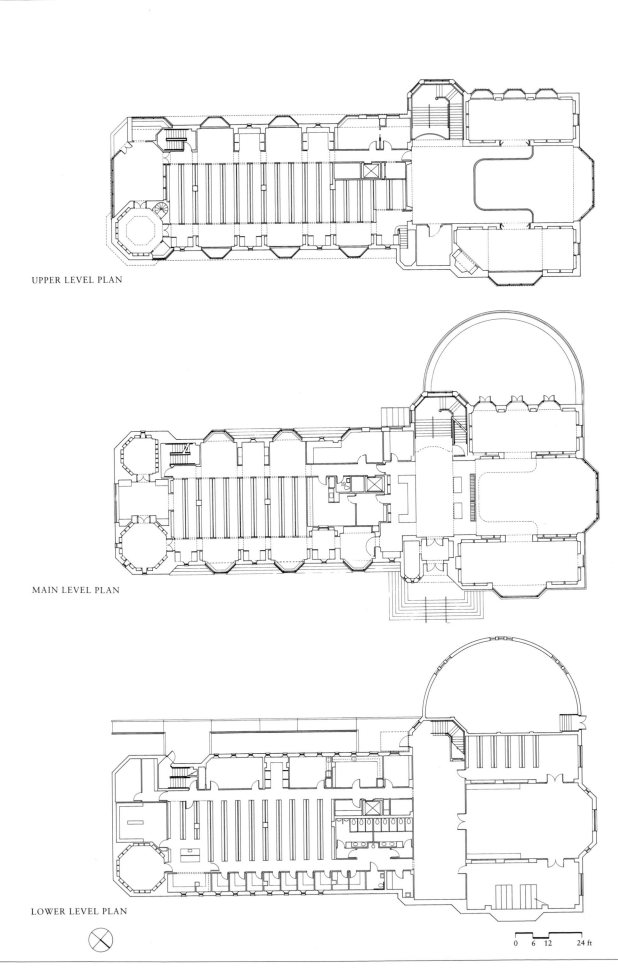

UPPER LEVEL PLAN

MAIN LEVEL PLAN

LOWER LEVEL PLAN

0 6 12   24 ft

9. Entrance hall
10. Neilson Reading Room
11. Kehaya Reading Room
12. Baker Reading Room
13. Ceiling of Baker Reading Room
14, 15. Principal stair

230

9

10

11

12

13

14

15

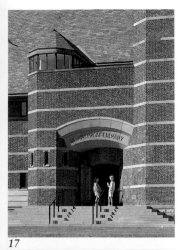

17

18

19

16. View from Chapel of St.
    Peter and St. Paul
17. Entrance portal
18. Weathervane
19. East facade
20. View from Baker Reading
    Room of Lower School
    Pond
21. View across Lower School
    Pond

20

Woodlynne

Birmingham, Michigan
1987–91

236 Woodlynne attempts to continue the tradition of prewar suburban developments in which land was not merely subdivided but was developed to establish a visually coherent neighborhood. Woodlynne is a twenty-four-acre portion of a former estate in Bingham Farm, Michigan, on which fourteen semi-custom-designed houses, ranging from 4,500–6,000 square feet, will be built.

Two houses have been built to date. One, on Lot 3, with brick walls and low-pitched, hipped and shingled roofs, reflects a characteristic midwestern vernacular that has its origins in such early work of Frank Lloyd Wright as his Winslow House (River Forest, Illinois, 1893). The second house, on Lot 14, has been developed along with extensive gardens to evoke English models like Lutyens's Tigbourne Court. The house thus fits into a local tradition that can be seen at its best in Albert Kahn's Cranbrook House (1907), in the neighboring village of Bloomfield Hills.

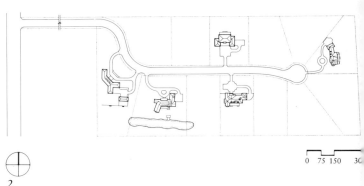

1

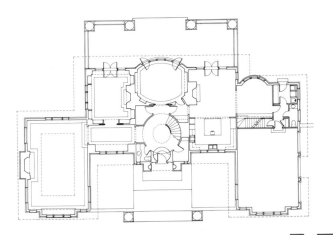

0 75 150 30

2

0 5 10 20

3

4

5

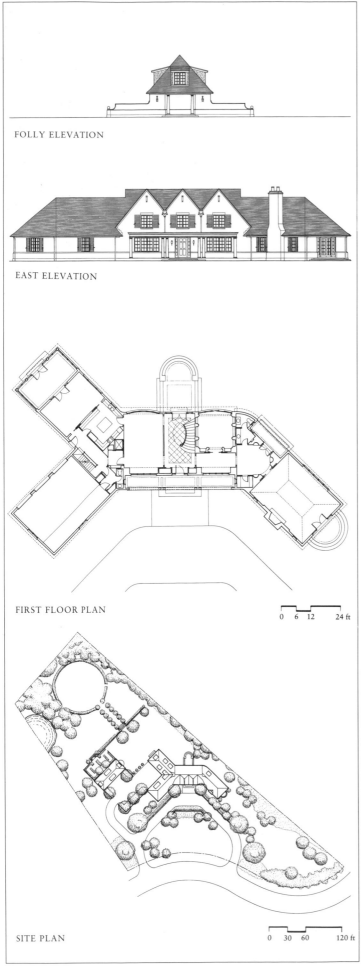

FOLLY ELEVATION

EAST ELEVATION

FIRST FLOOR PLAN

0 6 12 24 ft

SITE PLAN

0 30 60 120 ft

7

8

9

THE GABLES

6. Elevations and plans
7. View from garden to screened porch
8. Oblique view of southwest facade
9. View through garden gate
10. View from east
11. Living room
12. Principal stair

10

11

12

The Norman Rockwell Museum at Stockbridge

*Stockbridge, Massachusetts
1987–92*

240

Drawing on the simple classicism of New England's traditional public buildings, this design seeks to accommodate the complex programmatic elements of a modern museum within a facility that has the scale and directness that Norman Rockwell's art represents.

The site is part of the former Butler estate (1859), the principal buildings of which were built in a style more typically associated with villas in the Hudson River Valley. To enhance the experience of Rockwell's art without compromising the character of the early buildings on the site, the approach is designed so that the arriving visitor does not see the villa, but passes across a surrogate village green—the grassy enclosure of a former cutting garden—to find the museum's cupola-crowned entrance porch, which is the only break in the screen of white pine and spruce. Inside, the museum is organized to provide the visitor with a clear path of circulation and a clear sequence of well-lit gallery spaces. The main galleries, intended for permanent installations, are naturally top-lit, with supplementary artificial sources of illumination; other galleries, intended for changing exhibitions and works on paper, rely exclusively on artificial light sources.

At the building's heart, an octagonal gallery, top-lit by a lantern, is dedicated to Rockwell's paintings of the Four Freedoms. A cross-axis opens up to a view of the terrace that overlooks the Housatonic River Valley. At this point, as visitors stroll along a path leading to Rockwell's studio, which has been relocated to the site from Stockbridge Village, they are given a glimpse of the Butler villa, now housing offices for the museum staff.

1. *Site plan*
2. *Principal plan*
3. *Perspective of museum approach*
4. *Perspective of Four Freedoms gallery*
5. *Perspective of barrel-vaulted gallery*

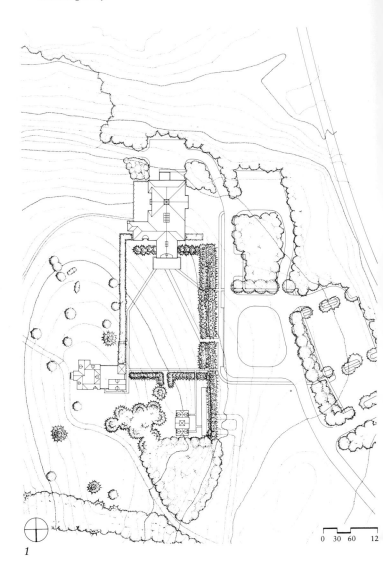

1

0 30 60   12

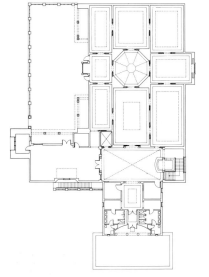

0 12 24   48

2

3

4

5

Disney's Yacht and Beach Club Resorts Walt Disney World

*Lake Buena Vista, Florida
1987–91*

YACHT CLUB
1. *Entrance gatehouse*
2. *View from Stormalong Bay*
3. *View from lake looking east*
4. *View across canal to entrance*

242   Two hotels—with a combined total of 1,215 guest rooms, a 110,000-square-foot convention center, and a 35,000-square-foot "fantasy" pool—make up this resort complex adjacent to the EPCOT Center at Walt Disney World.

While both hotels draw their inspiration from America's architectural past, each has a unique identity. The Yacht Club is reminiscent of the rambling, shingle-covered seaside resorts that were built toward the end of the last century in New England towns such as Newport, Marblehead, and Bar Harbor. The Beach Club is lighter, more airy in expression. It is modeled on the many Stick Style cottages and resorts that were found in towns like Cape May, New Jersey.

1

2

3

244

CONVENTION
CENTER

BEACH CLUB

YACHT CLUB

LAKE

KEY PLAN

0   75   150   300 ft

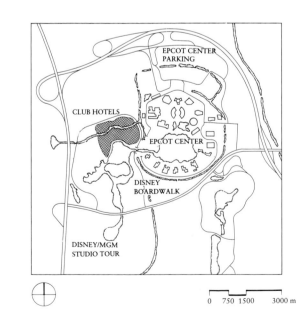

EPCOT CENTER
PARKING

CLUB HOTELS

EPCOT CENTER

DISNEY
BOARDWALK

DISNEY/MGM
STUDIO TOUR

SITE PLAN

0   750 1500   3000 m

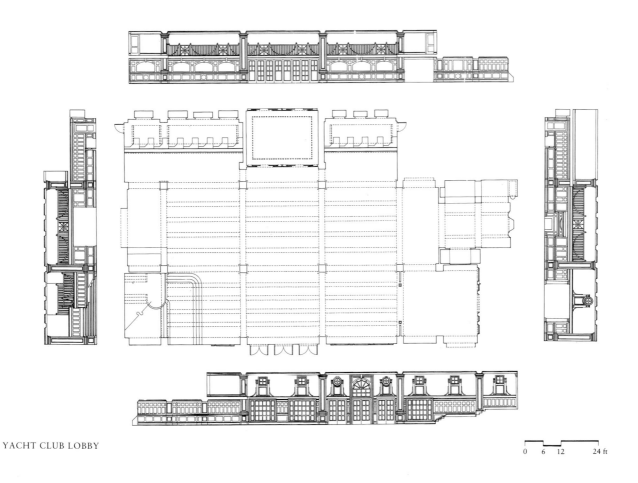

YACHT CLUB LOBBY

0   6   12   24 ft

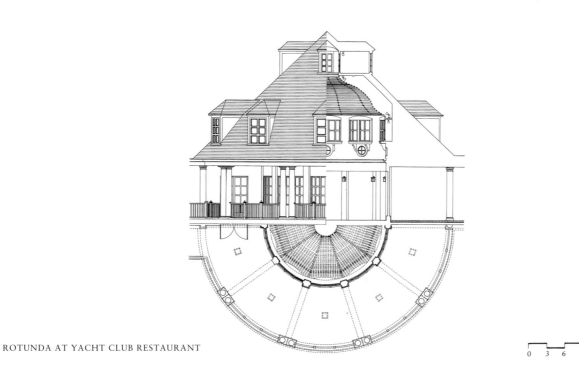

ROTUNDA AT YACHT CLUB RESTAURANT

0   3   6   12 ft

7

8

9

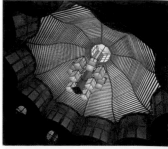

10

11

YACHT CLUB
7. *Veranda*
8. *Lobby*
9. *Yachtsman's Steakhouse*
10. *Detail of restaurant ceiling*
11. *Typical guest room corridor*
12. *View from southwest*

BEACH CLUB
13. *View from southeast*

12

13

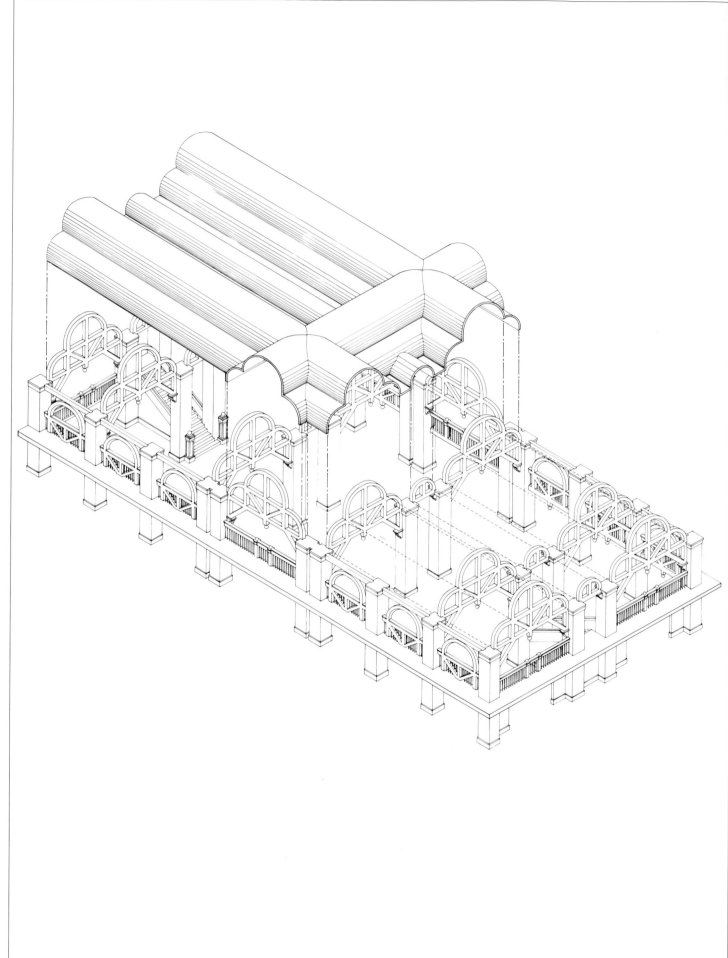

BEACH CLUB

14. *Lobby axonometric*
15. *Lobby elevations and
    reflected ceiling plan*

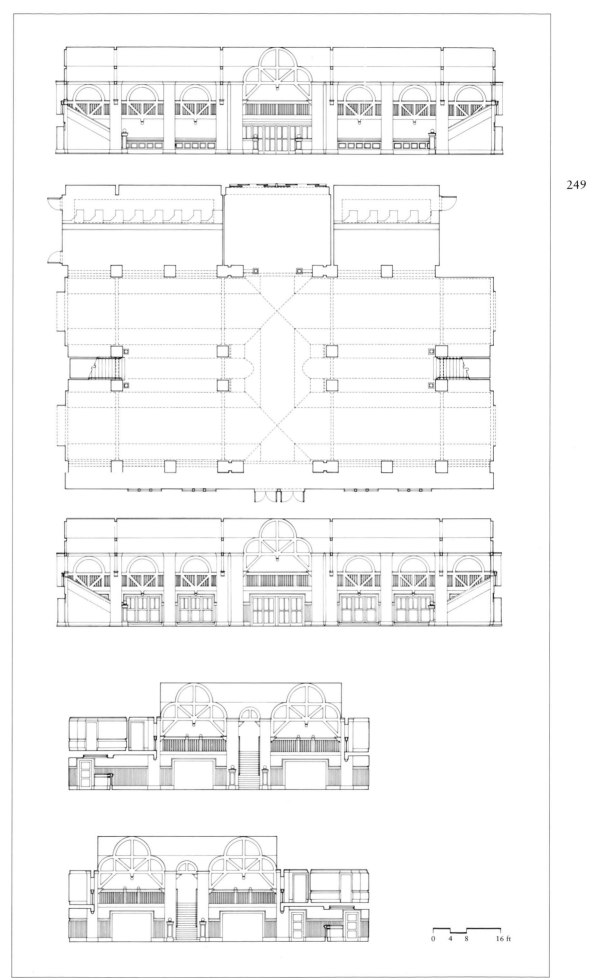

0 4 8   16 ft

16

17

18

19

20

BEACH CLUB
16. *Aerial view from Yacht Club looking east*
17. *Lakeside Cannae Court entrance*
18. *Quiet Pool elevation*
19. *Entrance and porte cochere from northwest*
20. *Detail of veranda*
21. *Entrance and porte cochere*
22. *Lobby*
23. *Newport Suite*

21

22

23

CONVENTION CENTER
24. *Plans and elevations*
25. *Approach from south*
26. *Entrance lobby*
27. *Pre-convention gallery*
28. *Night view of Club Hotels*

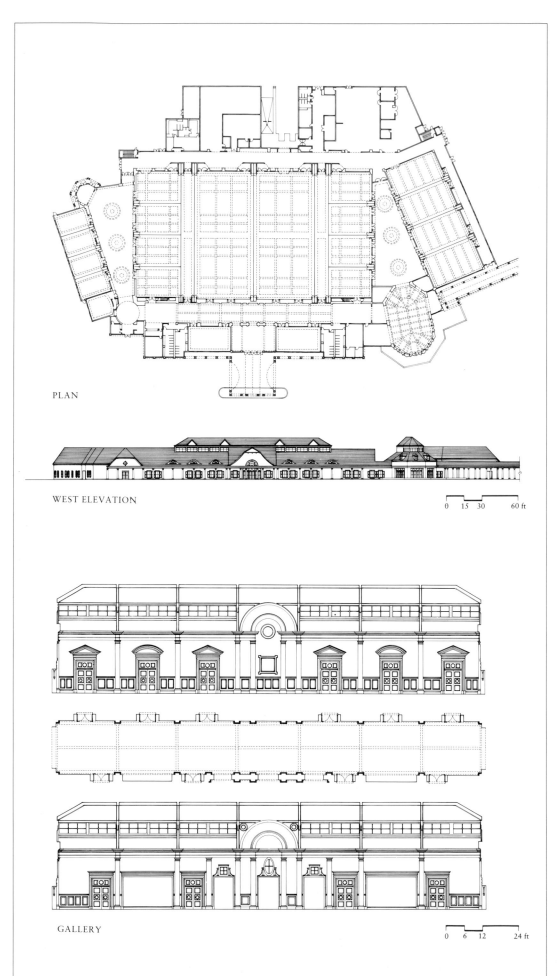

PLAN

WEST ELEVATION

0 15 30   60 ft

GALLERY

0 6 12   24 ft

25

26

27

Ninety Tremont Street

Boston, Massachusetts
1988–90

1. *Tremont Street elevation*
2. *Section*
3. *Perspective along Tremont Street*

256 This project combines the restoration and modernization of the Tremont Temple Baptist Church (Clarence Blackall and George Newton, 1894), to be undertaken by others, with the creation of a new office building atop the temple and on an adjacent corner site to the south.

The design was conceived as two related masses. The principal mass, reaching a height of 170 feet, is treated in the classical manner, with a clearly defined base, shaft, and top. The first two stories maintain the rustication of the neighboring temple facade. Eighth- and ninth-story setbacks help ensure that the temple's pediment facade will retain its distinctive profile. The secondary mass is a horizontal, fly-loft-like penthouse atop the temple. This portion of the composition, also 170 feet high, is set well back from the temple's facade—twenty-five feet for most of its height and an additional two feet at the height of the adjacent Parker House Hotel extension.

In contrast to the temple, with its richly polychromed decorative patterning conceived by Blackall to suggest the subtleties of a watercolor wash, Ninety Tremont Street incorporates austere coursed limestone and precast facades that relate to the classicism typical of downtown Boston's best commercial buildings.

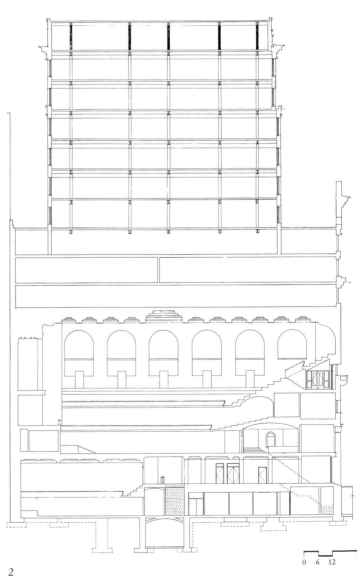

1

0 15 30 6

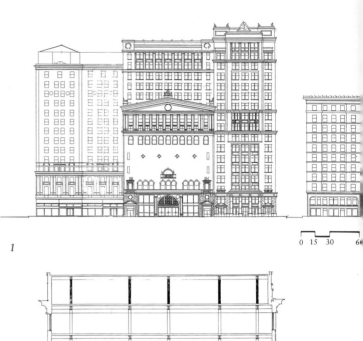

2

0 6 12 2

Banana Republic

Chicago, Illinois
1990–91

1. *North Michigan Avenue facade*
2. *View from northeast*
3. *View from southeast*

258 Moving beyond the elephants, jeeps, and army-surplus fatigues of its Mill Valley, California, origins, Banana Republic commissioned a new freestanding, two-story prototype store on a prime site on Chicago's North Michigan Avenue. The themes of travel and the tropics remain, but Banana Republic's new jungle is represented rather than reproduced.

Conceived as a contemporary version of a tropical plantation villa, the lead-coated copper and bronze facade recalls the prefabricated metal structures exported to jungle colonies from Europe in the late nineteenth century. Inside, where a plantation villa is suggested in the plan of roomlike bays surrounding a glazed double-height courtyard, the mood is warmer, with wood, carpet, and leather combined. Under the skylight, a suspended glass and steel stair provides the main focus. The jungle image is also evoked with lacquered particle-board tents lashed with steel cable. But specially designed tables, racks, and display cases reflect the essential modernity of the design concept, also apparent in other aspects of the project.

1

2

260

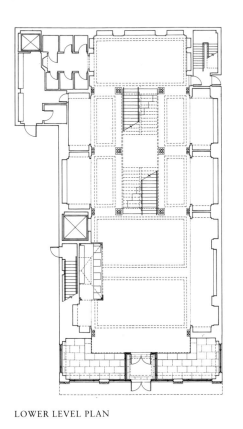

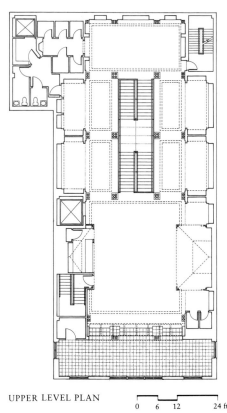

LOWER LEVEL PLAN

UPPER LEVEL PLAN

0   6   12   24 ft

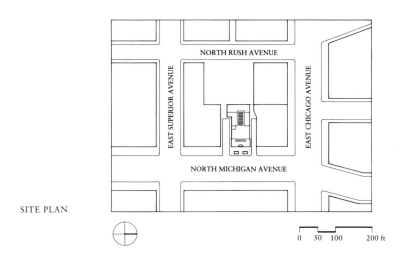

SITE PLAN

NORTH RUSH AVENUE

EAST SUPERIOR AVENUE

EAST CHICAGO AVENUE

NORTH MICHIGAN AVENUE

0   50   100   200 ft

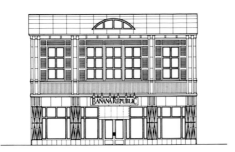

EAST ELEVATION

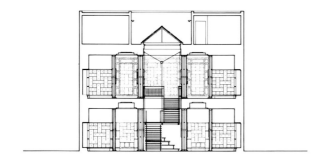

NORTH-SOUTH SECTION LOOKING EAST

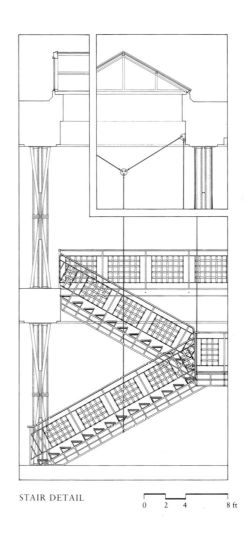

STAIR DETAIL

0   2   4   8 ft

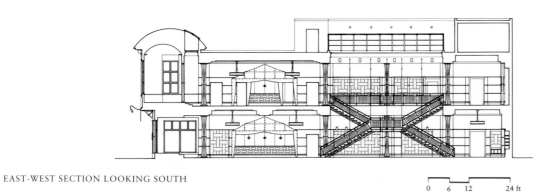

EAST-WEST SECTION LOOKING SOUTH

0   6   12   24 ft

262

6

7

8

9

Apartment House

Chicago, Illinois
1989–

264 Located near Chicago's Lincoln Park, this fourteen-story apartment house contains twenty-three apartments ranging in size from 3,000 to 4,500 square feet. Modeled after luxury buildings characteristic of the pre–World War II era, each apartment has a 600-square-foot living room, a formal dining room, a library, a family room, a gallery, two to five bedrooms, a powder room, a laundry, a maid's bath, and a cedar closet for off-season storage. The building has several setbacks beginning at the eleventh floor, with terraces at each of the units. Terrace apartments include a full-floor penthouse and a five-bedroom duplex.

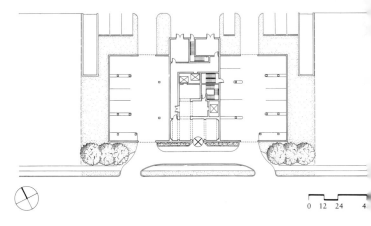

1

2

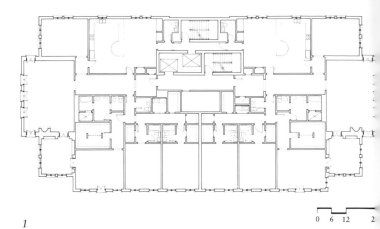

3   4

Denver Public Library Competition

Denver, Colorado
1990–91

266 This design was developed for a three-way competition for the expansion and renovation of the Central Library, designed in 1955 by Burnham Hoyt. The 400,000 square feet of new facilities will be added to 100,000 square feet of renovations to the existing library. In its use of materials, setback massing, and fenestration, this addition builds on the design vocabulary of Hoyt's building while at the same time introducing new elements such as a 140-foot tower, a south-facing arcade, and new materials like buff-colored Colorado sandstone.

The seam between the old and the new building, a sixty-foot-wide, five-story-high Grand Hall lit by clerestory windows, contains escalators that connect all the public floors. At the uppermost level of the Grand Hall is the library's western history collection, where a special reading room faces west toward the Rocky Mountains.

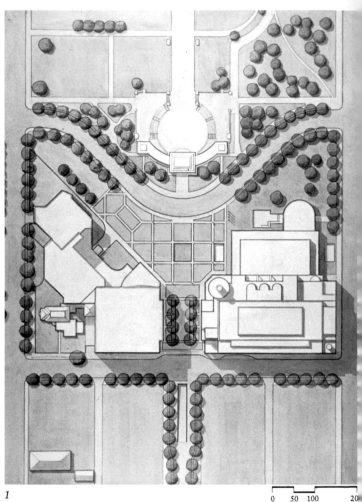

1

0   50   100   200

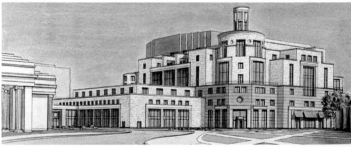

2

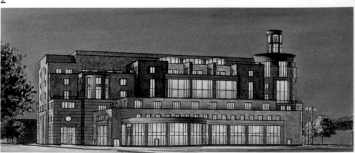

3

4

5

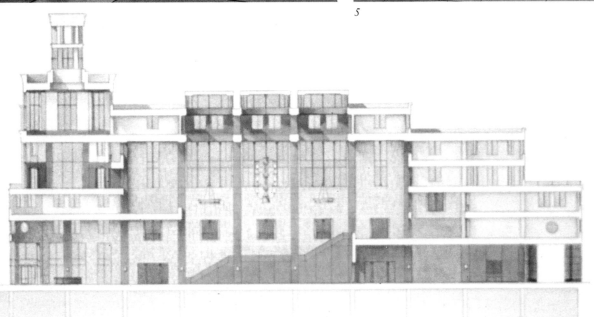

6

0   12   24   48 ft

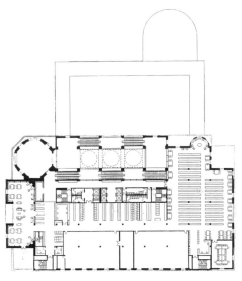

FIFTH FLOOR PLAN

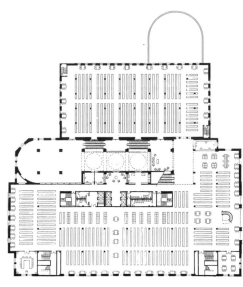

SECOND FLOOR PLAN

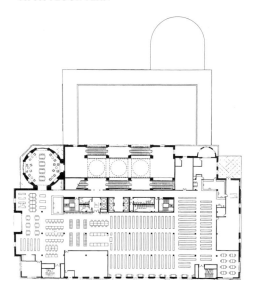

FOURTH FLOOR PLAN

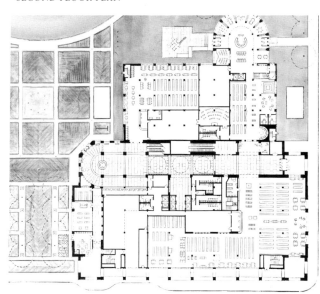

GROUND FLOOR PLAN

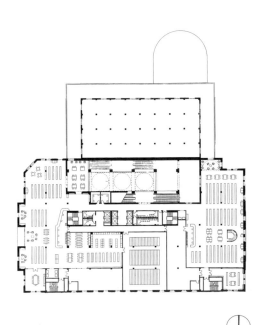

THIRD FLOOR PLAN

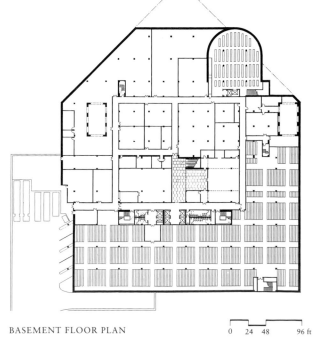

BASEMENT FLOOR PLAN

0   24   48   96 ft

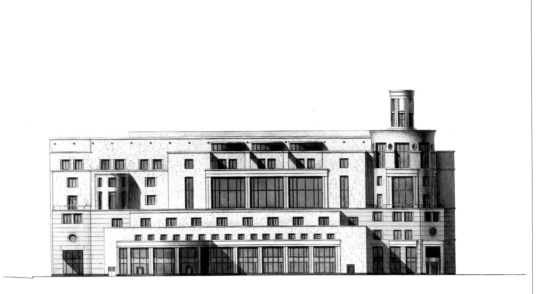

NORTH ELEVATION

SOUTH ELEVATION

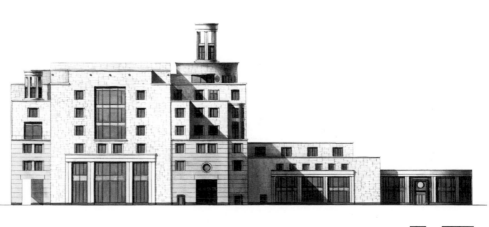

EAST ELEVATION

0 12 24   48 ft

Columbus Regional Hospital

Columbus, Indiana
1988–93

1. West elevation
2. Site plan
3. South elevation

270   Founded in 1917 as the Bartholomew County Hospital on a site just beyond the town center, this hospital had grown in a piecemeal fashion to its current 400,000 square feet. Because the hospital had not utilized the land it had acquired over the years, by the mid-1980s it was squeezed into one corner of a thirty-eight-acre site bisected by Haw Creek. At best, the existing facility could be described as a haphazard collection of buildings of various sizes and degrees of functional obsolescence. The only architecturally notable building, the original Italianate structure, was the least worthy of preservation, since it was functionally outmoded.

This master plan reorients the hospital. A new entry drive spans Haw Creek on a new bridge, uniting the two halves of the site. Flanking the drive, almost as gatehouses, are two 30,000-square-foot medical office buildings. Also on the creek's western bank a new seventy-five-in-patient psychiatric facility is proposed, in close proximity to an existing outpatient facility.

Within the hospital itself, the master plan proposed the creation of a series of new two-story pavilions and intervening outdoor courtyards connected by a continuous double-height gallery. These pavilions provide individual identity and self-contained facilities for cancer care, physical and occupational therapy, and a women's center. Second-level bridges cross the public concourse to connect the pavilions to the hospital's surgery suite, one of two portions of the existing facility that will remain after the design is completed. The other portion to remain is the six-story patient tower, which is being upgraded inside, with an additional story and a half added at the top, and outside, with a completely new cladding.

The extensively glazed concourse contains registration and billing departments, a gift shop, and waiting areas for the various departments; it also links to the main entrance, the emergency suite, and a new cafeteria, which will be located in a glassy pavilion next to the entrance at the base of the bed tower.

1

2

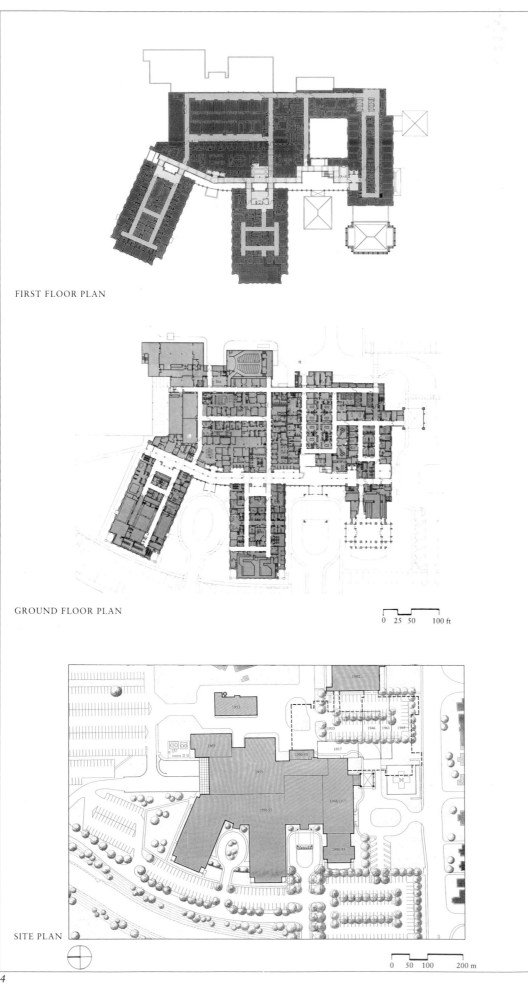

FIRST FLOOR PLAN

GROUND FLOOR PLAN

0   25 50   100 ft

SITE PLAN

0   50   100   200 m

4. Plans
5. Construction view from
   southwest
6. Perspective of gallery
   looking toward main lobby
7. Perspective of dining room

5

6

7

Hotel Cheyenne
Euro Disney

Marne-la-Vallée, France
1988–92

274   This 1,000-room hotel is organized as a complex of two-story buildings conceived in the image of a nineteenth-century American western town, but filtered through the lens of Hollywood. Unlike its prototype, which has a hotel as just one of the buildings along Main Street, the Hotel Cheyenne is the town itself. At the principal crossroads, where a street leads across a creek to the Hotel Santa Fe, there is a restaurant and check-in building.

While the streets of typical western towns ran in straight lines and opened to endless vistas of prairie and mountains, the streets of Hotel Cheyenne, like those of the "back-lot" western towns built by Hollywood studios, have vistas angled to screen out "backstage" areas from the cameramen and the actors, who in this case are one and the same—the hotel guests.

1. *View of Main Street from Desperado Square*
2. *View of main entry building*
3. *Lobby*
4. *Guest services desk*

1

2

3

4

276

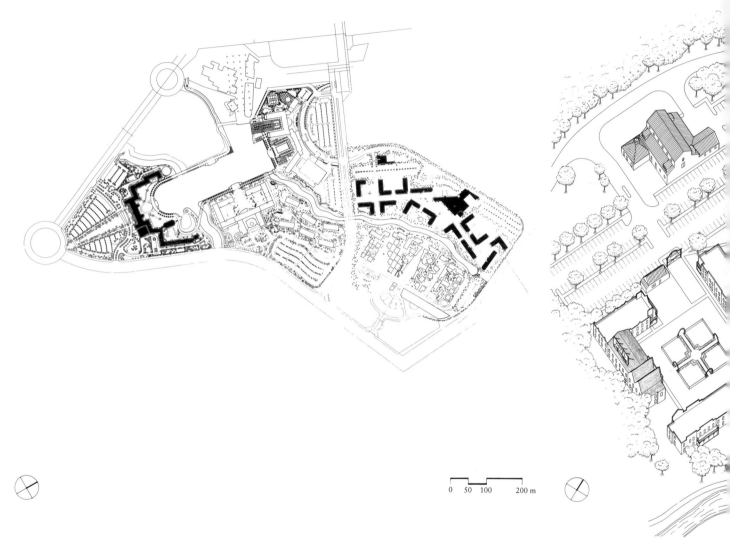

0 50 100   200 m

5

6

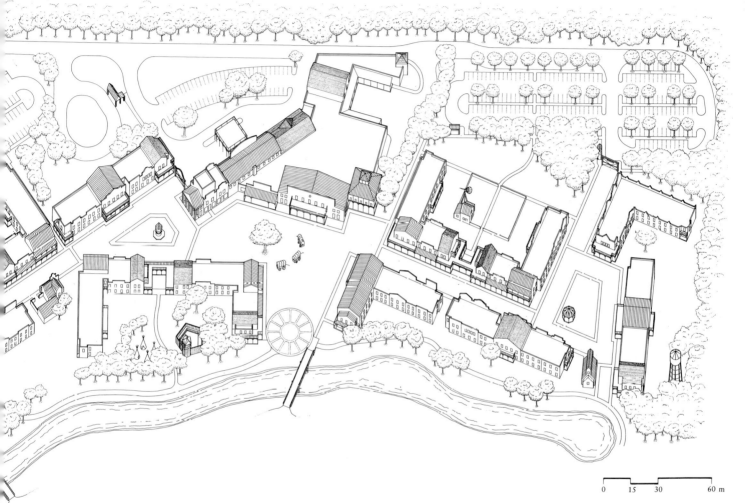

0   15   30   60 m

Newport Bay Club Hotel
Euro Disney

Marne-la-Vallée, France
1988–92

1

2

278 The 1,098-room Newport Bay Club Hotel evokes the tradition of grand American resorts, in particular that of Shingle Style seaside hotels along the northeast coast. Glimpsed across a lawn from the *rond point*, its 730-foot-long colonnaded porch is the symbolic gateway to the resort portion of Euro Disneyland.

Arriving guests walk from the porte cochere into a painted, wood-paneled lobby and lounge, both providing direct views to the lake, which during the summer will be dotted with small paddleboats and sailboats. From the lobby and lounge, a staircase leads below to two restaurants that in warm weather open out onto the garden terrace.

More informal than the front, the sprawling lakeside elevations of the hotel are punctuated by a profusion of figural elements that help break down the scale: towers, pergolas, dormers, and a lighthouse. To center the composition, a giant gambrel pediment serves as the culmination of the lake's axis.

1. *Detail of entrance*
2. *Porte cochere*
3. *Lobby*
4. *Cape Cod Restaurant*
5. *Entrance facade*

3

4

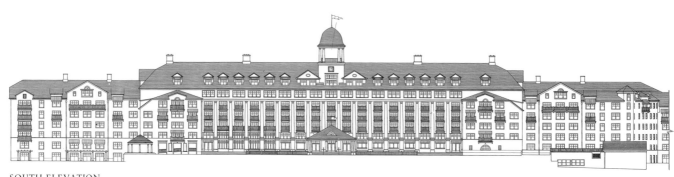

SOUTH ELEVATION

NORTH ELEVATION

0 4 8   16 m

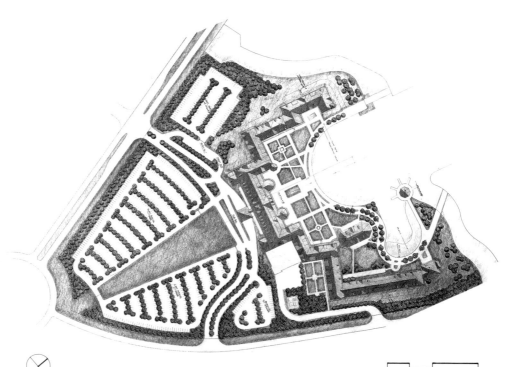

SITE PLAN

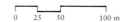

0   25   50   100 m

281

7

8

9

10

Residence at Briar Patch

East Hampton, New York
1984–91

1. *Section facing east*
2. *Site plan*
3. *View from west*
4. *View from southeast*
5. *Pool and poolhouse*

284   Wetland restrictions influenced the firm's decision to nestle the house at the southeast corner of its wooded, two-acre property. The house is approached along a drive that is kept to minimum dimensions to allow a small swimming pool and cabana to be slipped in on one side. The simple gable-ended principal mass of the house forms an ell with the service wing, enclosing a defined entrance court. On the opposite side, a broad dining porch is cut into the mass to take advantage of a pond view. Inside, a center hall opens onto the staircase and the living and dining rooms, creating an expansive interior landscape.

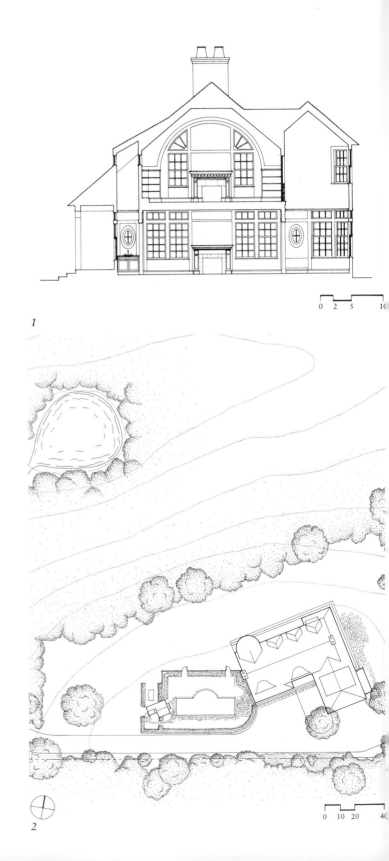

0 2 5 10

1

0 10 20 40

2

3

4

5

Nittsu Fujimi Land
Golf Club

Izu Peninsula, Japan
1988

286   The Izu Peninsula, with its proximity to
both Tokyo and Mount Fuji and its
temperate climate, is a premier location
for prestigious golf clubs. Situated on a
beautiful but steeply sloping site, the
Nittsu Fujimi Land Golf Club enjoys
views of Mount Fuji and Sagami Bay. The
image of the clubhouse is of a grand villa
complete with a belvedere set in a rolling
landscape. The principal rooms—the
lounge, the dining room, and the executive
rooms—are oriented to the views, while
the more private areas—the meeting
rooms and bathing areas—overlook
intimate courtyards.

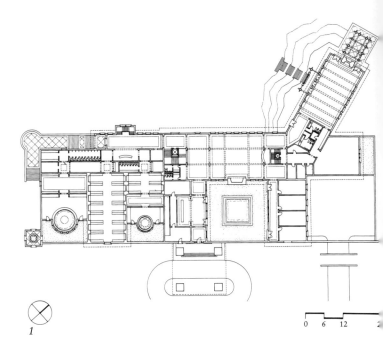

1

0   6   12

2

3

Na Pali Haweo

Oahu, Hawaii
1990–

288   Na Pali Haweo, a ridge development located east of Hawaii Kai and directly north of Koko Head, offers views both east to Molokai and west to Diamond Head and downtown Honolulu beyond. The brief was to design a signature park and a gatehouse at the entrance to the development and eight houses set around a cul-de-sac to the east overlooking the park. The houses were organized as a hillside village, the picturesque broken silhouette of which complements the varied topography and the intricacies of the predetermined view corridors.

To date, the only portions of the development to be realized as designed are the park and the gate. The gate consists of a pair of obelisks and a long, low, wisteria-covered pergola set in a backdrop of bougainvillea trees located to either side of the entrance road, which winds its way through an existing nondescript subdivision. The park, located at the foot of the Na Pali Haweo estate and to the east side of the entrance road, presents a singular image: an allee of Washingtonia palms set against a semicircular lawn. Within the lawn are a number of shady monkey-pod trees, and around its perimeter are a pavilion and a wisteria-covered pergola recalling the language of the gateway at the bottom of the hill.

1

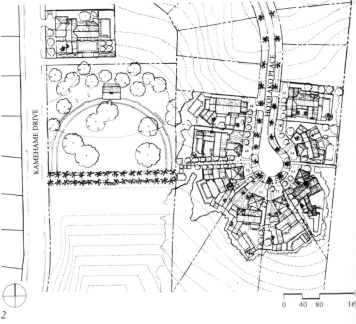

2

3

4

Brooklyn Law School Tower

Brooklyn, New York
1986–93

290   The new campanile-like tower provides the ninety-year-old Brooklyn Law School with expanded facilities and an image in keeping with its long history and growing reputation. Located directly across from the recently renovated Brooklyn Borough Hall (Gamaliel King, 1846–51), the tower visually establishes the law school as a component in the borough's traditional civic center, which also includes on an adjacent site the Municipal Building (McKenzie, Voorhees & Gmelin, 1926), from which the design takes many cues.

The first nine floors of the new tower are connected to those of the existing building. They provide upgraded and expanded student and faculty facilities, including lecture and seminar rooms, libraries, and a cafeteria. A formal dining room is located on the tenth floor, and a faculty library is on the eleventh. In addition to the 85,000 square feet of new space, the project involves the renovation of 65,000 square feet in the existing building, including the redesign of classrooms and moot court.

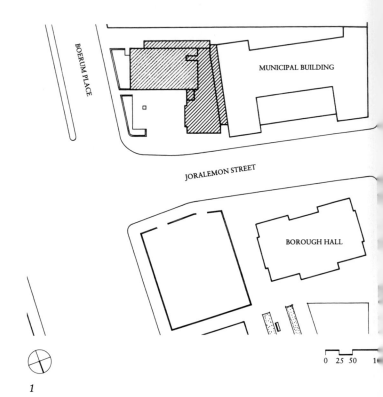

1

1. Site plan
2. Joralemon Street elevation
3. Study model of library
   check-out lobby
4. Study model of cafeteria

2

3

4

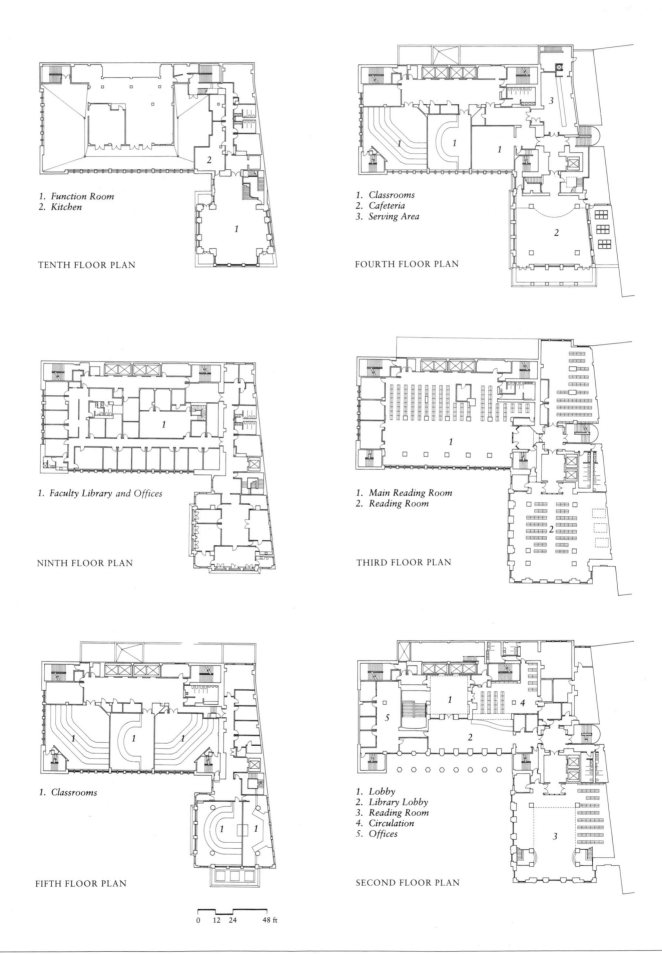

1. Function Room
2. Kitchen

TENTH FLOOR PLAN

1. Classrooms
2. Cafeteria
3. Serving Area

FOURTH FLOOR PLAN

1. Faculty Library and Offices

NINTH FLOOR PLAN

1. Main Reading Room
2. Reading Room

THIRD FLOOR PLAN

1. Classrooms

FIFTH FLOOR PLAN

1. Lobby
2. Library Lobby
3. Reading Room
4. Circulation
5. Offices

SECOND FLOOR PLAN

0   12   24   48 ft

JORALEMON STREET ELEVATION

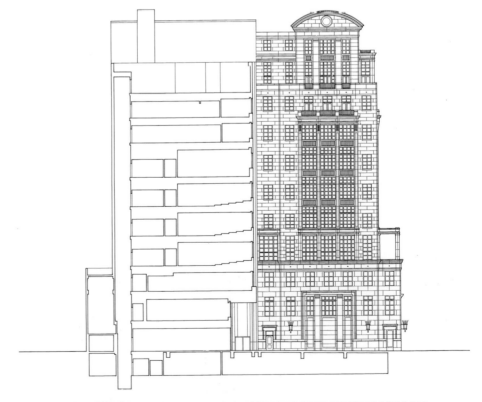

BOERUM PLACE ELEVATION AND SECTION THROUGH EXISTING BUILDING

0   9   18   36 ft

Residence in River Oaks

Houston, Texas
1986–92

294 This house occupies one of the last remaining undeveloped sites in the planned suburb of River Oaks. In an effort to reconcile the site's northern view toward the Buffalo Bayou with the desire to have direct southern light in the principal rooms facing the entry side, courtyards were designed to buffer the south-facing rooms from the driveways. To the north, formal gardens extend the geometry of the house into the landscape.

Creamy stuccoed walls and red tile roofs were chosen because they work equally well in Houston's intense sun and gray rainy season. They also evoke the Mediterranean influences seen in some of the area's most interesting architecture. Pavilionated planning, local symmetries of massing, and a decorative vocabulary of Tuscan details governed by Doric proportions combine to lighten the effect and help reduce the apparent size of the house.

1. *Scheme two, entrance elevation*
2. *Scheme two, view from garden*
3. *Scheme one, entrance elevation*

1

2

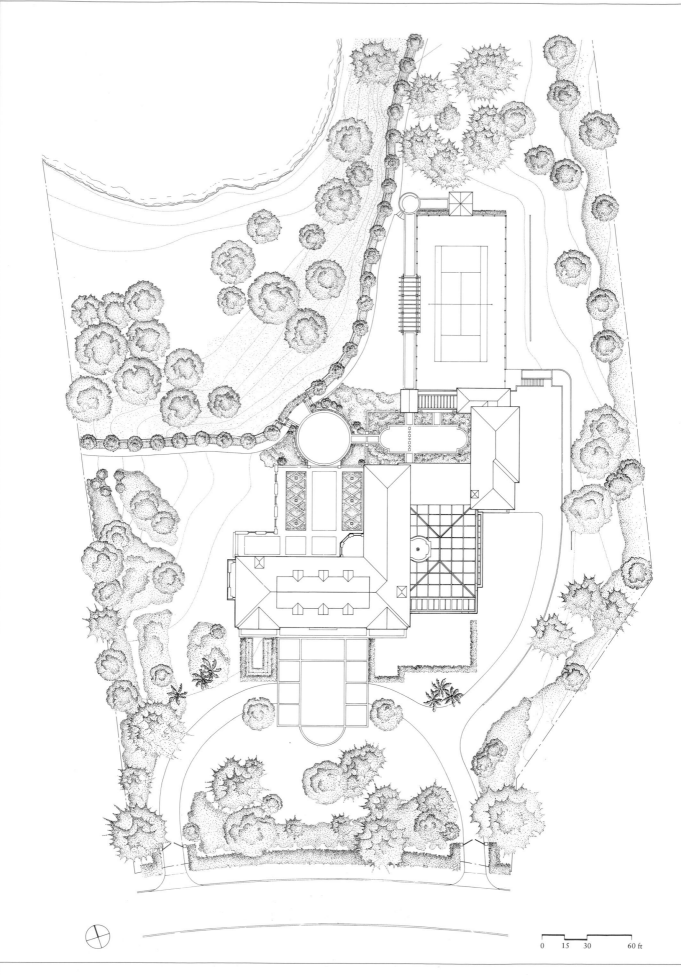

0 15 30   60 ft

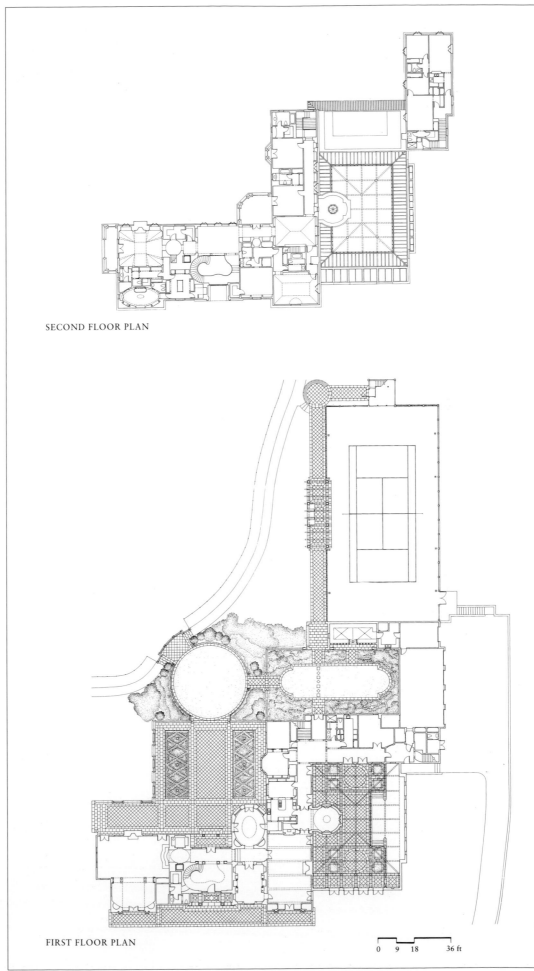

SECOND FLOOR PLAN

FIRST FLOOR PLAN

0 9 18   36 ft

Chiburi Lake Golf Resort

Chiburi, Japan
1990–

298 Set in the rolling hills of Tochigi
Prefecture, this golf resort offers a variety
of distant views toward surrounding
mountains. The firm's contribution to the
resort consists of condominiums located
on two sites that flank a hotel/golf
clubhouse, being designed by others.

In order to vary the scale of the buildings,
to create a broken, picturesque skyline, to
form exterior courtyards, and above all to
create a sense of individuality for the
dwelling units, the design varies in length
and height from one to four stories. It also
incorporates a wide variety of
architectural elements such as gables and
hips of various sizes, porches and
balconies, pergolas and terraces, and
chimneys, as well as contrasting but
compatible materials, such as stone,
stucco, and wood.

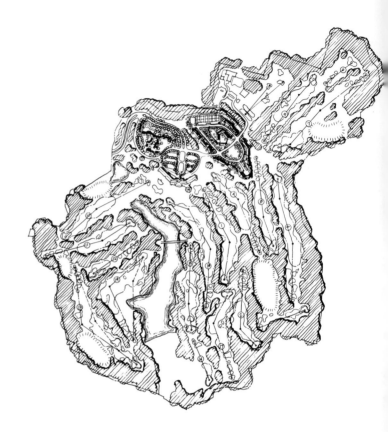

1

0 50 100 2

2

3

4

GROUND FLOOR PLAN

SOUTH ELEVATION

0 10 20   40 m

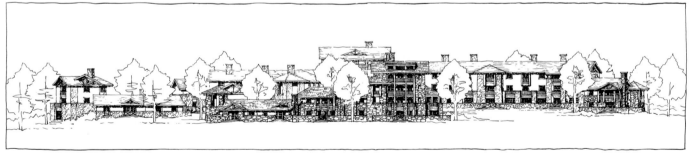

SOUTH ELEVATION

NORTH ELEVATION

0   5   10   20 m

GROUND FLOOR PLAN

SOUTH ELEVATION

0 10 20   40 m

PARK ELEVATION

TENNIS COURT ELEVATION

0   5   10   20 m

Kitsuregawa Golf Club House and Inn

Tochigi Prefecture, Japan
1990–

302 Heavily wooded rolling hills and rice fields provide the setting for this golf resort. A winding entrance road leads to the clubhouse, which is set on the highest hill on the site, and continues on, via a bridge, to the inn on a neighboring hill to the southwest.

The campanile of the villalike clubhouse can be seen from all points on the golf course, while long, low-pitched roof wings embrace the landscape, creating courtyard and terrace areas that offer more intimate views.

The villagelike inn consists of a number of buildings: the inn itself, an executive villa, and ten guest villas, all overlooking a man-made pond with a view of the clubhouse beyond to the northeast. The main room of the inn is the dining hall, in effect a bridge that connects one side of the pond to the other and offers guests distinct views to the north and south.

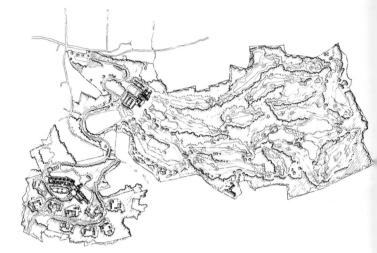

1

0 100 200   4

2

3

4

ENTRANCE ELEVATION

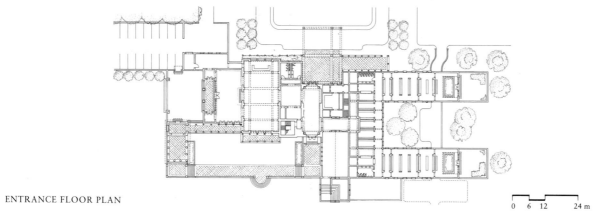

GOLF COURSE ELEVATION

ENTRANCE FLOOR PLAN

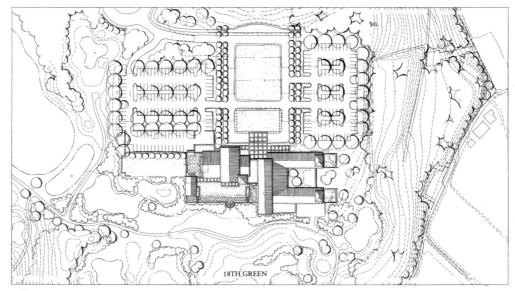

SITE PLAN

18TH GREEN

ENTRANCE ELEVATION

GARDEN ELEVATION

0   5   10   20 m

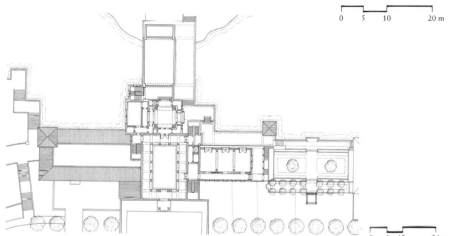

ENTRANCE FLOOR PLAN

0   6   12   24 m

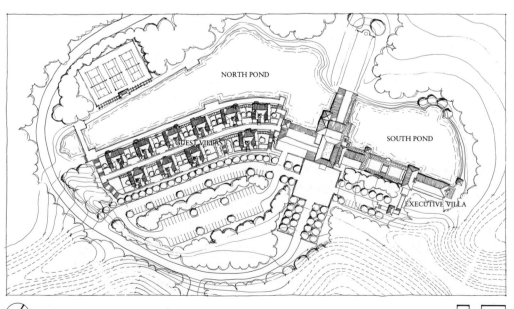

NORTH POND

SOUTH POND

GUEST VILLAS

EXECUTIVE VILLA

SITE PLAN

0   10   20   40 m

Roger Tory Peterson Institute

Jamestown, New York
1989–

306   A center for the study of ornithology in particular and the natural sciences in general, the newly established institute is mandated to serve visiting scholars, educators, and small groups from the public at large. Its headquarters, to be realized in stages, will eventually contain a broad range of facilities. The first stage will consist of a public gallery for the exhibition of wildlife art; an archive for the preservation of wildlife art and rare books on the natural sciences; a library; meeting and conference rooms; and offices. The second stage will include natural history field-service space consisting of an observation gallery, equipped with telescopes and microphones for close examination of nature, and lab rooms for specimen inspection and categorization; paths through five ecological sub-systems; an auditorium; a shop; seminar rooms; and additional administrative space.

The environmental commitment of the institute is reflected in the picturesque massing and rustic vocabulary of the new building.

1

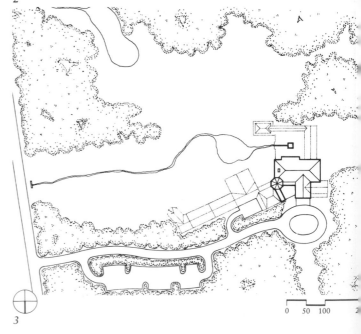

2

3

0   50   100

4

5

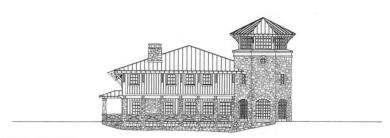

EAST ELEVATION

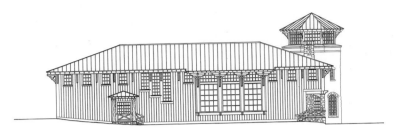

SOUTH ELEVATION

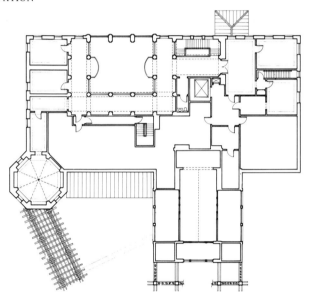

SECOND FLOOR PLAN

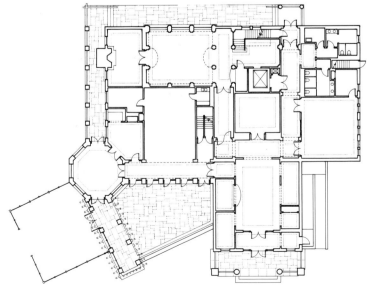

FIRST FLOOR PLAN

0   8   16   32 ft

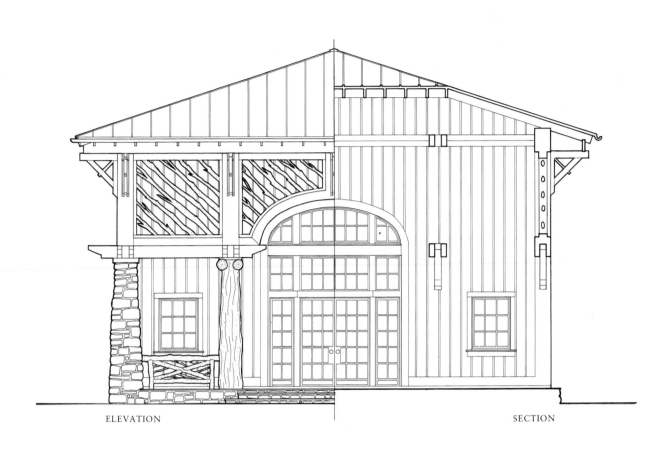

ELEVATION   SECTION

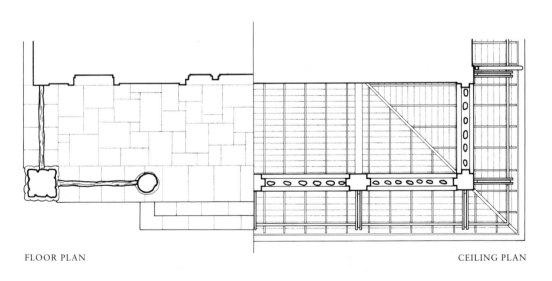

FLOOR PLAN   CEILING PLAN

0   2   4   8 ft

Residence in North York

Ontario, Canada
1988–

310   Occupying a double lot in one of metropolitan Toronto's oldest suburbs, this slate-roofed, rubble-stone design evokes some of the architecture surrounding the site as well as more elaborately realized American examples of French-inspired suburban houses such as those designed by Mellor, Meigs and Howe, and Robert Rodes McGoodwin.

The composition of semidiscrete pavilions, designed symmetrically about a central mass yet asymmetrically offset by the cottagelike projecting guest wing, not only contributes to the picturesque aspect of the exterior but also serves to reduce the house's apparent bulk. Development of the site concentrates on the front and rear yards, while the sides remain narrow buffers against the neighboring houses. In pointed juxtaposition to the more public nature of the front motor court, the rear garden has been designed as a sequence of landscaped "rooms" increasing in intimacy as they descend to a courtyard that provides access to the lower-level indoor pool.

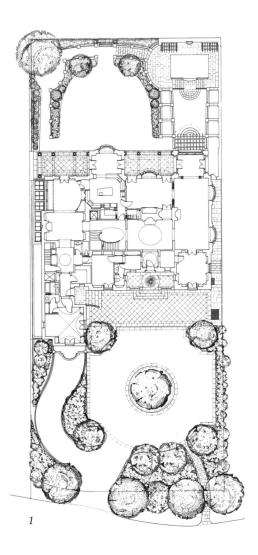

1

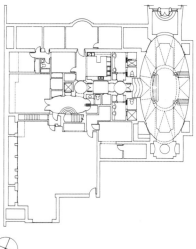

2

0   8   16   32 ft

3

4

5

0　8　16　　　　32 ft

The Center for Jewish Life
Princeton University

Princeton, New Jersey
1986–93

312   Located at the corner of Ivy Lane and Washington Road, the street separating Princeton's academic campus from the residentially scaled district containing the eating clubs of Prospect Street, the Center for Jewish Life combines religious and social functions within a comfortable, clublike setting. Although the center was initially designed as two wings added to an existing house, an entirely new building was designed based on the old parti when the existing house proved structurally unsound. The building contains offices, a library, lounge space, a dining room, and a sanctuary—the center's principal religious space—which will be supplemented by the auditorium and library, allowing simultaneous services for each of the three branches of the Jewish faith.

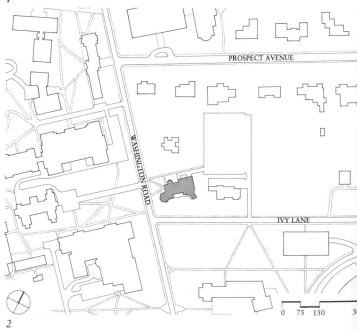

1

2

ANDREW ZEGA, DEL. 1991

1. *Reception Office*
2. *Sanctuary*
3. *Classroom*
4. *Lounge*
5. *Dining Room*
6. *Private Dining*
7. *Serving Area*
8. *Kitchens*

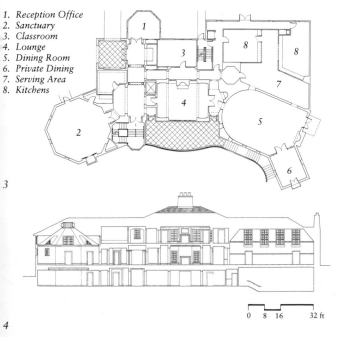

3

4

0 8 16   32 ft

5

West Village Golf Resort

Tochigi Prefecture, Japan
1990–

314   The site, set within wooded rolling hills, is about one and a half hours by Bullet Train north of Tokyo. A hundred-room resort hotel is to be built in stages. In the first stage, there will be forty rooms as well as a championship-quality clubhouse for the two golf courses, served by a common lobby. To facilitate staging, and to avoid the institutional look of many contemporary resorts, the building has been organized as a set of pavilions arranged around a series of water elements, with the clubhouse facing south, where it will overlook the 18th hole, and the hotel facing west, where it will take advantage of distant mountain views.

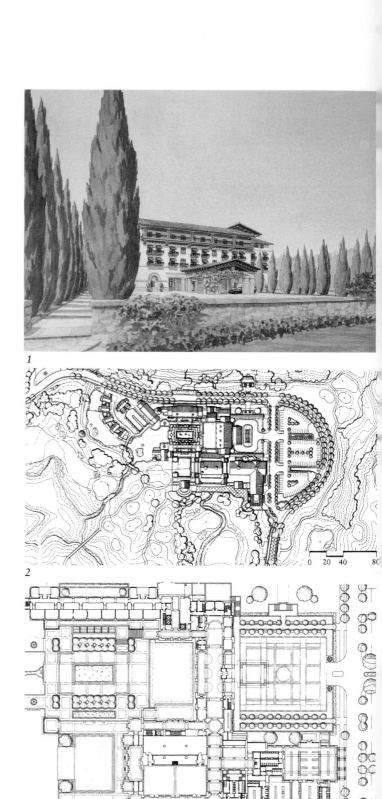

1

2

3

315

4

5

0   10   20   40 m

Izumidai Resort

Izu Peninsula, Japan
1990–

316 This dramatically steep site offers views of Itoh City, Sagami Bay, and surrounding hills, as well as a distant view of Mount Fuji. A tree-lined public road winds through the site, connecting a five-story resort hotel with one- to five-story residential condominiums and landscape and recreational features such as a pond and a small community park.

To organize and articulate the complex, the hotel was conceived of as a hilltop villa and the housing as a hillside village. Bridging a ravine, the hotel consists of two principal elements: the main building, with fifty guest rooms, restaurants, and banquet facilities; and a connected one-story recreational wing, accessible from the main lobby, incorporating a swimming pool, bathing/spa facilities, and a bar-lounge. Both building elements are arranged around courtyards to maximize southern light and privacy while taking advantage of the sweeping views to the north.

The 320-unit residential village is organized around three courtyards, each distinct in character in terms of size, height of the surrounding buildings, and landscaping: the courtyards are conceived of as a water court, a flower court, and an English meadow. At the center of the village is the community house, which has a bolder scale that visually refers to the hotel on the hill.

1

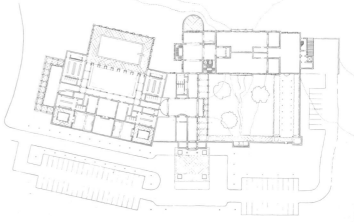

0 10 20

5

Residence in
Hunting Valley

Geauga County, Ohio
1990–92

1. *Garden elevation*
2. *Site plan*
3. *First floor plan*
4. *North elevation*

318   This house occupies a wooded knoll in the horse country outside Cleveland, Ohio. A long, low, rambling mass of shingled walls, flared roofs, and broadly overhanging porches recalls the countrified Shingle Style designs of such practitioners as William Ralph Emerson, as well as the Western Reserve style characteristic of local farmhouses. The general informality of the exterior is contradicted at one point by a Greek Doric colonnade that anchors the principal covered porch to establish a dignity in keeping with its commanding position overlooking a pond being created in the meadow below.

The linear plan leads from a double-height, barrel-vaulted living hall, past dining and family rooms, to the owners' private quarters, which consist of a library and master-bedroom suite. The several skewed "legs" of the plan, devised to articulate the enfilade in relationship to functional requirements, come together in the combined family room/kitchen, at once the physical and social center of the house.

1

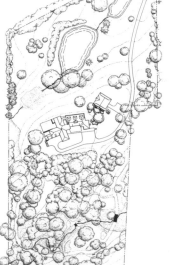

2

0 60 120   240

ANDREW ZEGA, DEL. 1991

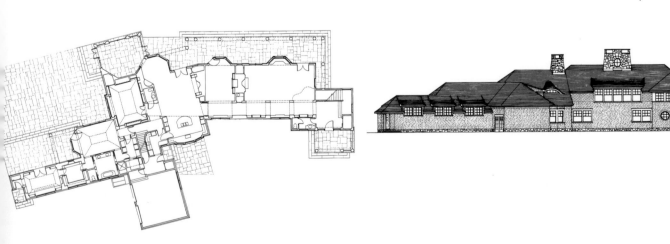

4

0 8 16   32 ft

The Turning Point Competition

Amstelveen, The Netherlands
1990–91

320 Located at the important intersection of Rijkswega-9 and Keerpuntweg, this 129,000-square-foot office building and fifty-three-suite executive hotel is intended to stand as a prominent gateway to the Amsterdam suburb of Amstelveen. Breaking down a large development into a group of smaller, interconnected buildings, the design contrasts large elements with small and solids with voids, recalling the forms of a traditional town and providing the building's various tenants with distinct architectural identities. In their massing, the clustered buildings rise toward the northern edge of the triangular site, respectfully drawing away from the adjacent residential neighborhood and creating a sun-flooded, south-facing entry courtyard. Landscaped with abstract parterres of greensward and seasonal planting and provided with a cascading water wall, this courtyard creates an inviting approach to the building's four entrances while providing an amenity to the surrounding neighborhood. To the north and east a broad reflecting pond with landscaped banks buffers the site from two major roadways and from the tracks of a high-speed tramway. The irregularly angled juxtaposition of the building's various parts carefully responds to views from Burgermeister Rihnderslaan and from the exit ramp used by cars approaching the site from the direction of Amsterdam.

Through its detailing and use of materials the complex evokes both traditional Dutch building forms and the playful and idiosyncratic forms that characterize the architecture of the Amsterdam School and the early years of Dutch modernism. Carefully detailed brick walls of contrasting buff and red rise from a stone base. A combination of punched windows and prow-fronted bay windows adds interest, variety, and scale to the elevations. The sculptural use of vaulted roof forms further enhances the building's traditional, domestic, and uniquely Dutch character.

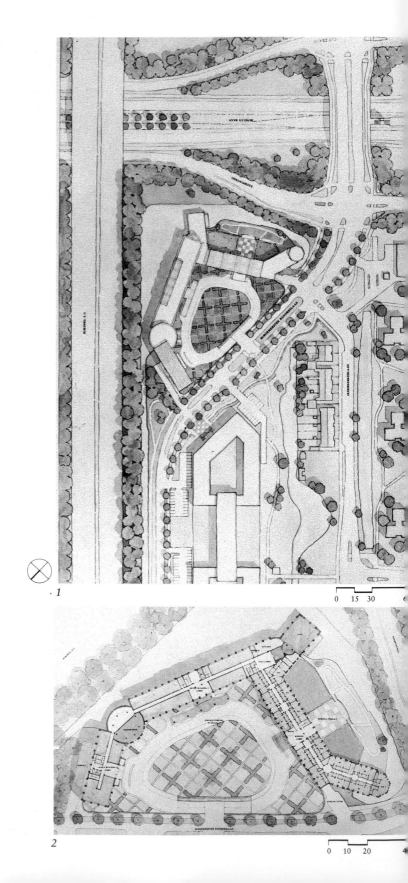

1

2

3

House at Apaquogue

East Hampton, New York
1989–93

322 Reflecting the owners' requirements for a classically inspired design that would fit into the local context, this house looks to Georgian prototypes, and especially to eighteenth- and early-nineteenth-century East Hampton houses, for its massing and detail.

The primary rooms are contained within a rectangular gambrel-roofed mass bracketed by identically sized, shed-roofed library and kitchen wings. To the north, the wing containing the family room and garage appears to be an earlier saltbox-type house to which the grander, symmetrical house was later added. Rough, thickly cut cedar shakes and bold classical moldings enliven the simple forms of the house, in contrast with the taut, machine-cut shingles and planar trim of the more picturesque forms of the Shingle Style. Large and small scale are vividly contrasted: giant pilasters bracket the central entry facade and support deep-bracketed eaves; slender, paired colonettes support the entry porch. Inside, the large rooms open onto one another, demonstrating the kind of country-house planning perfected at the beginning of this century, although the interior details again derive from earlier American prototypes.

1

2

0   45   90

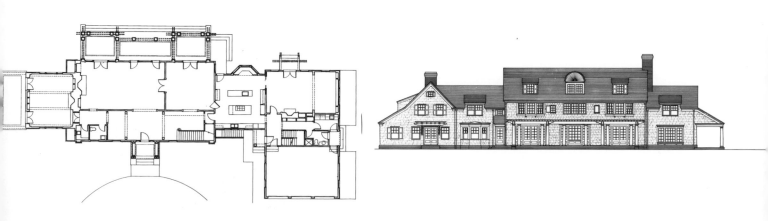

0 8 16 32 ft

Mountain Residence

Yamanashi Prefecture, Japan
1991–

324   The client's request for a square plan was the impetus for this Palladian-inspired villa. The site, 6,500 feet above sea level and set in wooded terrain on rolling hills, offers distant mountain views and a great deal of privacy. The combination of a long stone-base pergola and an open gable form creates a facade with a commanding presence, while the entrance and rose garden elevations are more low-key and intimate.

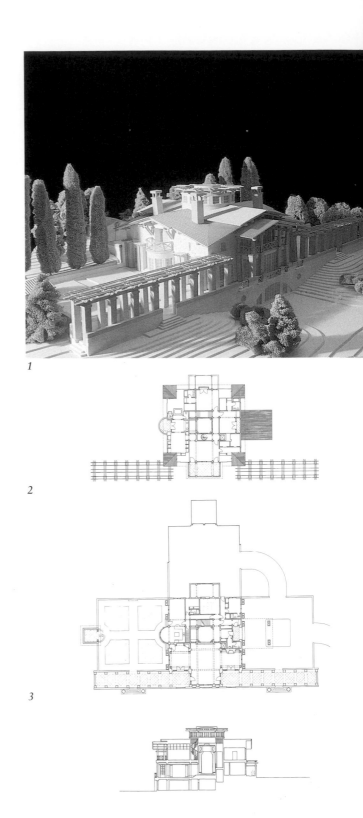

1

2

3

4

0   5   10   20 m

5

6

7

8

Tivoli Museum and Apartments

Tokyo, Japan
1991–

1. *Entrance elevation*
2. *Perspective from street*
3. *Location plan*

326 This three-story luxury apartment building located in Harajuku, in the heart of Tokyo, consists of seventeen apartments ranging in size from 640 to 2,900 square feet, 9,700 square feet of flexible office space on three below-grade levels, a small private museum, a restaurant with private dining facilities, and a rooftop garden and dining terrace. The building's massing—three stories above grade and three below—is determined by the site configuration, local setback and height limitations, and the total allowable building volume.

To maximize desirable light and views for the building's various public spaces, a water garden was located on the south side of the building; the water cascades down from a "temple grotto" to a reflecting pool below, offering a dramatic view from the circular entrance court. The court serves as the focal point for circulation to the building's various functions and is designed as a vertical sequence of water fountains originating above smooth stone columns and culminating in a serene pool.

1

2

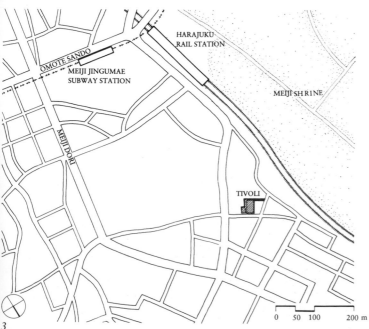

OMOTE SANDO

HARAJUKU
RAIL STATION

MEIJI JINGUMAE
SUBWAY STATION

MEIJI SHRINE

MEIJI DORI

TIVOLI

0   50   100   200 m

3

328

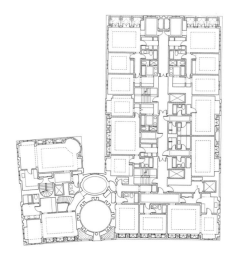

1. *Winter Garden*
2. *Spa*
3. *Garden Promenade*
4. *Music Podium*

ROOF PLAN

APARTMENT LEVEL PLAN

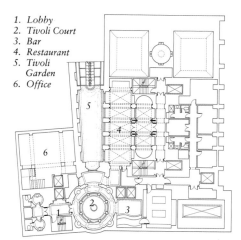

1. *Lobby*
2. *Tivoli Court*
3. *Bar*
4. *Restaurant*
5. *Tivoli Garden*
6. *Office*

RESTAURANT LEVEL PLAN

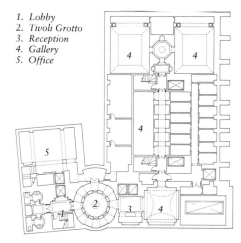

1. *Lobby*
2. *Tivoli Grotto*
3. *Reception*
4. *Gallery*
5. *Office*

MUSEUM LEVEL PLAN

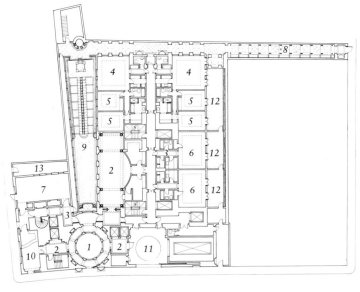

1. *Tivoli Court*
2. *Lobby*
3. *Entrance*
4. *Living Room*
5. *Bedroom*
6. *Studio*
7. *Office*
8. *Arbor Walk*
9. *Tivoli Garden*
10. *Gift Shop*
11. *Motor Court*
12. *Private Garden*

0   5   10   20 m

ENTRANCE LEVEL PLAN

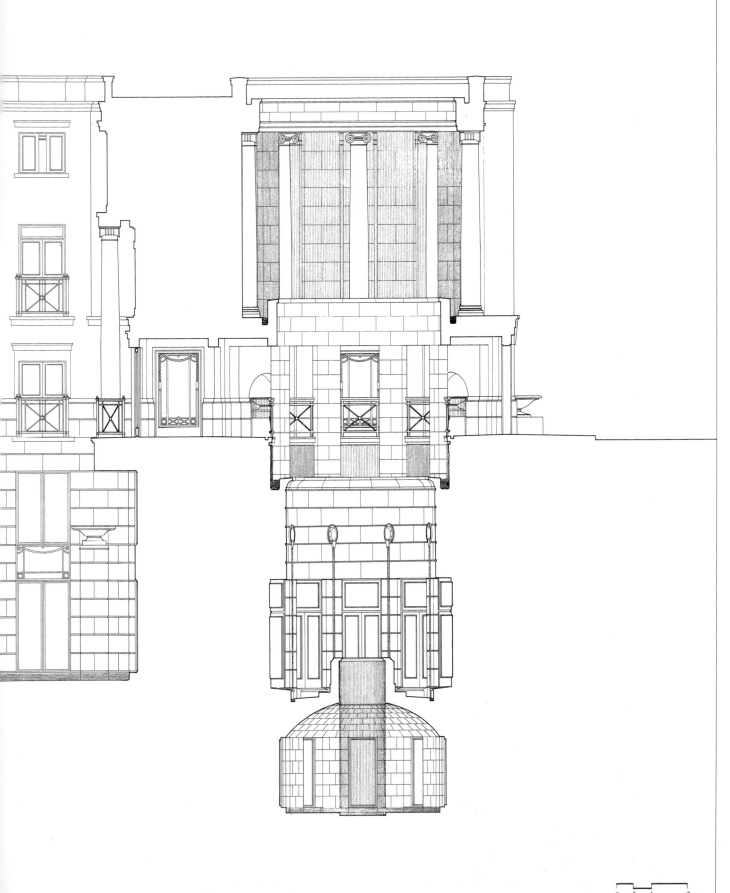

0   .5   1   2 m

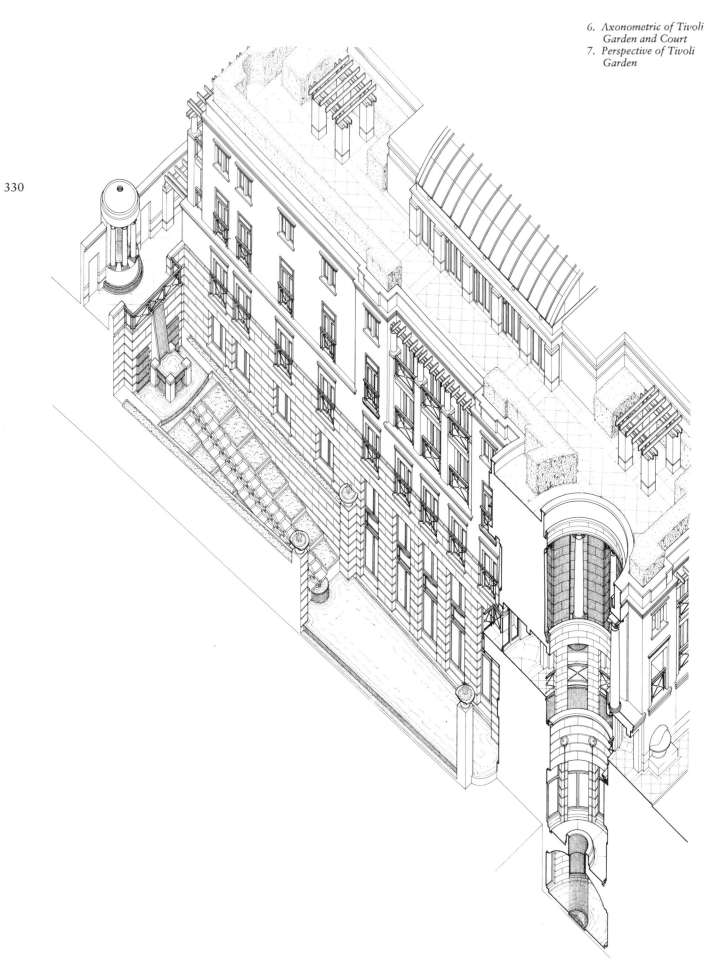

6. Axonometric of Tivoli
   Garden and Court
7. Perspective of Tivoli
   Garden

Del Mar Civic Center

Del Mar, California
1990

332   Our design provides for both the physical accommodation and the symbolic manifestation of municipal government in a small oceanfront town that prides itself on a long tradition of participatory democracy. The one-and-a-half-acre site fronts on Camino del Mar, the town's "main street," and slopes steeply toward the Pacific Ocean, three blocks to the west. A 10,000-square-foot city hall and 8,000-square-foot public library on Camino del Mar frame a gently sloping mid-block plaza. The casually angled placement of these buildings focuses the plaza on the entrance to the town's 250-seat meeting hall while allowing views to the ocean beyond. At the site's northwest corner, a plaza accommodates public parking during the week and an open-air farmer's market on Saturdays. Eighty-eight parking spaces are located at a lower level beneath the city hall and library.

The buildings share a relaxed palette that combines stucco walls with a brick base, wood trim, and a cedar-shingle roof. The use of hipped and pedimented roofs, wide eaves, and porticoed entrances recalls the architecture of the adjacent residential neighborhood and adds a note of civic permanence and grandeur.

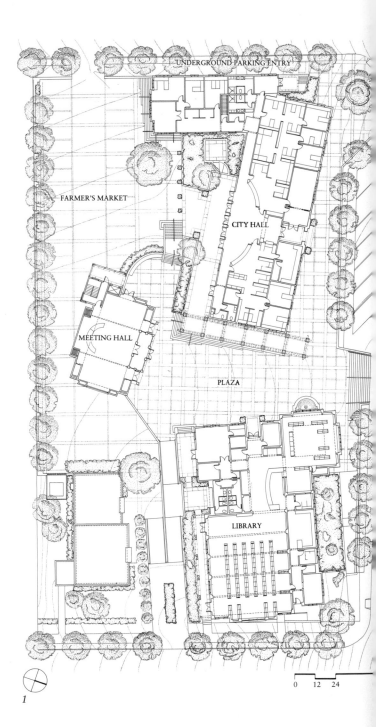

1

0   12   24

Entry plaza level plan
Perspective of community
plaza
Perspective of City Hall
plaza
Perspective of library

America House
The United States Embassy
Cultural and Consular Annex

Budapest, Hungary
1989–

334 In response to increasingly rigorous security criteria adopted for all United States embassies, the Department of State's Office of Foreign Buildings Operations has recently proposed the division of certain embassies into two separate parts: a secure component housing all classified activities, and a component housing all publicly accessible, non-classified activities. America House in Budapest represents one of the first of these publicly accessible facilities.

A six-story, 73,000-square-foot building located on Bajcsy Zsilinsky Ut, a prominent boulevard in Budapest's historic center, America House combines a series of public meeting, reception, and exhibition rooms on the ground floor with consular and commercial sections, as well as the library and offices of the United States Information Agency, on upper floors. In its exterior massing and appearance, the building is articulated into two parts: an office block reflecting the Secessionist classicism that flourished in Budapest in the two decades before the First World War; and a low-domed, Jefferson-inspired pavilion that marks the entrance and houses the library's principal reading room, providing a highly visible, symbolically charged, and distinctly American component.

1

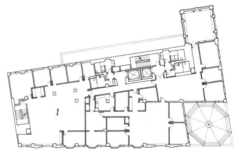

1. *Offices*

2

1. *Reference Room*
2. *Reading Room*
3. *Offices*
4. *Classroom*

3

1. *Entry Rotunda*
2. *Multipurpose Roo[m]*
3. *Exhibit Hall*
4. *Commissary*

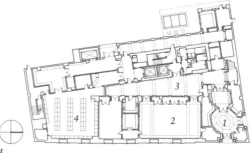

4

0   5   10

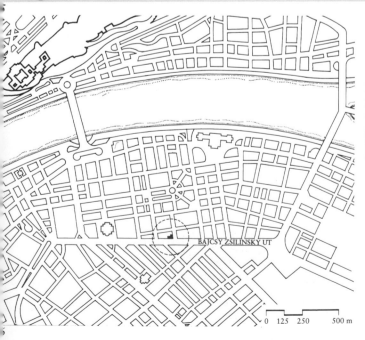

BAJCSY ZSILINSKY UT

0 125 250   500 m

Brooks School Library

North Andover, Massachusetts
1991–

Located among the gently rolling meadows of a nineteenth-century gentleman's farm, the Brooks School has grown since its founding in 1926 to become a 300-student, coeducational boarding school with the comfortable, domestic scale of a New England village. The firm's design for the school's new 21,000-square-foot library constitutes the first step in a long-term plan. Set at the campus's academic heart, the building required the realignment of the campus's main drive, the relocation of an existing administration building, and the unobtrusive accommodation of twenty-eight new, appropriately located parking spaces.

Because of its sloping site the library is entered at mid-level, where a centrally located circulation desk and staff area open to reference and periodical rooms and to a double-height, fifty-seat main reading room with windows facing the meadowed hillside and the distant forest beyond. Adjacent book stacks conceal small tables and carrels for private study.

In its architectural expression the building mirrors the clean simplicity of the original campus. Walls of white-painted brick with wood trim and operable double-hung windows rise to roofs of Vermont slate.

1

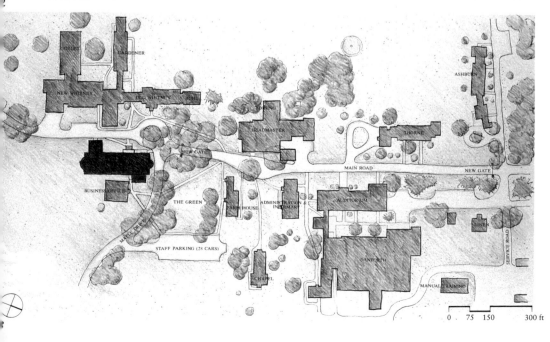

Darden School of Business
University of Virginia

Charlottesville, Virginia
1992–

338 The design for the new Darden School, located on the north grounds of the university, provides for both the physical accommodation and the symbolic manifestation of the school as it grows and enters its fourth decade as an international leader in its field. Set, acropolis-like, atop the natural crest of its fifteen-acre site, the new Darden campus consists of a central commons building flanked by ranges of academic and faculty pavilions to the south and by the school's library and future auditorium to the north, thereby mirroring the villagelike scale and character of the university's central grounds. Like Thomas Jefferson's "academical village," the buildings of the new Darden are separate yet interlocked for convenience, efficiency, and sense of community.

In its architectural expression the new Darden School is based on the buildings of Jefferson, now so much the definition of Virginia's architectural persona. The compositional ideas and classical formal principles follow Jefferson's language and, where appropriate, lead back to the work of Andrea Palladio and the late-eighteenth-century French visionary architect Claude-Nicholas Ledoux, both of whom Jefferson admired and drew upon. Sandstruck Virginia red brick walls with clean detailing of white painted wood, limestone or native white marble rise to red metal roofs punctuated by cupolas and chimneys, which serve as functioning vents and skylights while adding scale and visual interest to the campus silhouette.

1. *Perspective of approach*
2. *Site plan*
3. *Perspective of academic quadrangle*

1

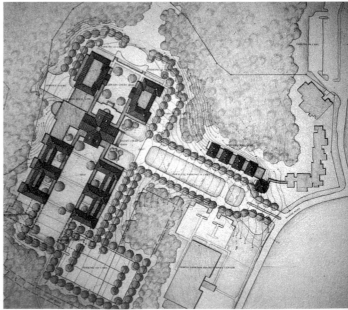

2

0 100 200

Additional Projects

Scarsdale Heights
Scarsdale, New York, 1984

This house is the first of nine that were to form the stylistically coherent developer-built community of Scarsdale Heights. The design vocabulary complements the Tudoresque flavor of the nearby 1920s Scarsdale Village.

Penthouse Apartment
New York, New York, 1984–85

Located in a banal postwar high-rise, this apartment features three sides that open to terraces, commanding expansive views along the East River. The classical plan, along with the abstracted vocabulary of classical detail, renders the space fixed and creates a sense of solidity and permanence.

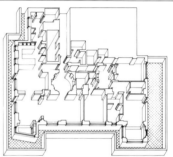

Russian Hill Townhouses
San Francisco, California, 1985

Three individually designed townhouses commanding panoramic views of San Francisco share a palette of materials, fenestration, and ornament common to the shingled architecture of Russian Hill, and especially to its near-neighbor, the firm's Russian Hill Residence of 1985–89.

Executive Suite, The Druker Company
Boston, Massachusetts, 1985–86

A tight space located at one corner of a larger office, the suite consists of a sitting room and an office finished in bubinga wood.

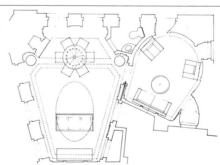

Milwin Farm
Ocean Township, New Jersey, 1985–86

The master plan for this fifty-acre site on a former estate provides for thirty-eight single-family houses, four of which were built to the firm's design, as was a gatehouse. The houses, each approximately 4,500 square feet in size, are sited to take advantage of the landscape features on the property while creating a coherent, villagelike group.

Addition to the Colonnade Hotel
Boston, Massachusetts, 1986

This twenty-story building, intended to completely fill in an open parcel, consists of a cylindrical tower that accommodates the narrowing of Huntington Avenue and provides a visual transition between the taller buildings of Copley Place and the long, low-lying slab of the hotel.

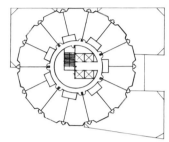

Craftsman Farms
Parsippany, New Jersey, 1986

Originally established on 1,000 acres in 1908, Craftsman Farms was the sylvan encampment of the furniture designer Gustav Stickley. This project called for fifty new houses to be built on the twenty-seven-acre parcel that remains undeveloped from the original estate, designed and sited in sympathy with the existing Stickley house and grounds.

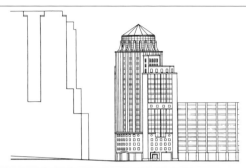

Residence
Wassenaar, The Netherlands, 1986

Situated in an established suburb of The Hague, this private residence incorporates a spacious floor plan within a solid, symmetrically composed exterior. In its massing, detailing, and materials, the house pays tribute to the fin-de-siècle architecture of the neighborhood and to the classicism of the Dutch Baroque.

Desert House
Phoenix, Arizona, 1986

Located on a steeply sloping site at the base of Camelback Mountain northeast of Phoenix, this house is composed of casually grouped templelike elements forming a series of courtyards and terraces.

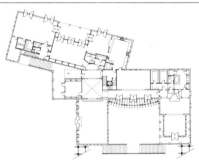

Ettl Farm Development
Princeton, New Jersey, 1986

This 184-acre development includes a combination of single-family houses and "manor" houses containing two to four condominiums, grouped close to roads to preserve maximum open space.

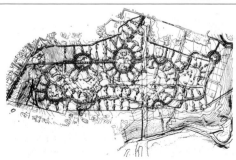

342

Essex Bay Estates
West Gloucester, Massachusetts, 1986

For a 290-acre former estate being developed into a 100-lot seaside community, three prototype houses were planned in the Shingle Style characteristic of the region.

Kiluna Farms
North Hills, New York, 1986

A series of prototype houses and outbuildings based on American Georgian models.

Two Newton Place
Newton, Massachusetts, 1984–87

This three-story, 110,000-square-foot brick and limestone office building complements Skidmore, Owings and Merrill's One Newton Place, which it faces, establishing a coherent yet varied new focus for the town's traditional commercial center.

Residence at Taylor's Creek
Southampton, New York, 1985–87

Located on a tidal pond, this house continues the tradition of picturesque estates characteristic of its immediate surroundings. In contrast to the verticality of the three-gabled entrance facade, the waterfront side of the house is less formal, with shed dormers, continuous eaves, and subsumed porches.

Upper East Side Apartment
New York, New York, 1986–87

While the existing space on the twenty-eighth floor of a new building was lacking in distinction, simple devices, such as panelized walls, large-scale moldings, and built-in cabinet work, transform the character of the apartment to yield a sense of spatial order and tectonic permanence.

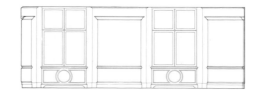

Winchester Country Club
Winchester, Virginia, 1987

This 25,000-square-foot building was proposed as a replacement for the outmoded facilities of an established country club.

Townhouse Apartment
New York, New York, 1987

This plan proposed to spatially and stylistically integrate a duplex apartment that long ago had been carved out of a brownstone.

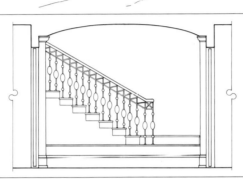

Sailors' Snug Harbor Music Halls Competition
Staten Island, New York, 1987

An extensive program called for the restoration and reuse of the Snug Harbor Music Hall (Robert Gibson, 1891), enlarging it to encompass a second 1,200-seat opera theater. This scheme proposed to build the theater in complementary fashion on the adjacent site.

The Grace Estate
East Hampton, New York, 1987

This development of thirty houses occupies more than 100 acres of a large, undeveloped, and secluded property surrounded by public reserve area and parkland. The house designs, one of which was built, follow a 100-year-old East Hampton tradition of shingled summer cottages.

Richmond Visitors' Center Competition
Richmond, Virginia, 1987

This winning but unrealized entry to a city-sponsored competition accommodates information and rest facilities as well as exhibition space to acquaint the visitor with the history and character of Richmond.

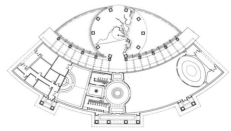

Santa Agueda Resort, Gran Canaria
Canary Islands, Spain, 1987

This contribution to the master planning of a proposed resort community of 30,000 people, to be located on a 1,300-acre site along the southern coast of Gran Canaria, focuses on the design of housing clusters and a hotel center.

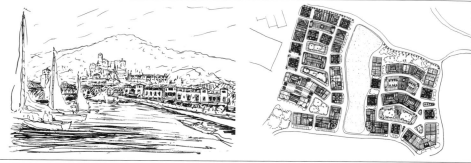

Pigeon Cove
Rockport, Massachusetts, 1987

A proposal for 100 apartment and townhouse units on a twenty-acre site a mile north of the picturesque town of Rockport.

New Town
Orlando, Florida, 1987

This planned residential community is designed as a traditional American town. Accommodating about 30,000 inhabitants, it consists of three villages, each with its own schools, shopping, recreation, and a variety of neighborhoods organized around small parks.

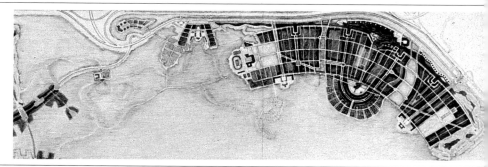

Patricof Apartment
New York, New York, 1982, 1986–88

A new connecting stair and a reworking of the plan recapture the lost Edwardian grandeur of an apartment in one of Park Avenue's oldest buildings.

Alterations and Additions to the Sunningdale Country Club
Scarsdale, New York, 1985–88

The addition doubles the size of the existing dining room, maximizes views, and provides access to the west terrace for summer sunset dining.

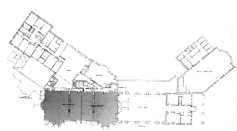

Middlesea Residence
East Hampton, New York, 1985–88

This house, on a site overlooking the Atlantic Ocean, is a renovation and expansion of a house built in 1930.

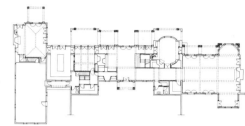

Renovations to a Residence in Edgartown
Martha's Vineyard, Massachusetts, 1986–88

A ranch-type house expanded and stylistically transformed.

Residence on Prospect Avenue
Hartford, Connecticut, 1986–88

This Regency-inspired house for a developer is placed on a long and narrow site justifying its rectangular massing. At the back, a glazed garden pavilion and a two-story glazed octagonal dining pavilion take advantage of the views of downtown Hartford.

Wynnewood Houses
Stamford, Connecticut, 1986–88

Occupying unused land of a former estate in North Stamford, Wynnewood consists of nine houses, two of which have been built, sited to take advantage of the property's woods and ponds and complement the 1930s colonial-style main house, which was retained as a residence.

Huppah for Temple Emanu-El
New York, New York, 1988

A traditional wedding canopy, carried on four bronze poles.

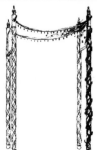

Bergdorf Goodman Window
New York, New York, 1988

In conjunction with the national convention of the American Institute of Architects held in New York in May 1988, Bergdorf Goodman, a Manhattan specialty store, invited ten architects to create store window displays for top fashion designers. This window featured the clothes of Geoffrey Beene.

Master Plan and Design, Colleges 9 and 10, University of California, Santa Cruz
Santa Cruz, California, 1988

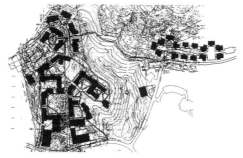

This scheme for Colleges 9 and 10 accommodates residential, recreational, and dining facilities for 1,500 students in addition to academic facilities for the economics, psychology, and anthropology departments.

Arrowwood Village
Ryebrook, New York, 1988

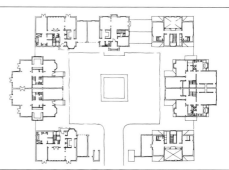

The client proposed to reduce the eighteen-hole golf course of an existing conference center to nine holes to accommodate 110 condominium units, each 2,800 square feet in size. The contrasting scales of the units and their varying shingled gables offer continuity of form and a picturesque silhouette.

Squaw Valley Master Plan and High Camp Ski Lodge
Squaw Valley, California, 1988

The master plan proposes a strategy for the phased construction of five hotels, 720 condominium units, and 200,000 square feet of retail space built on top of a two-story, semi-subterranean parking structure, as well as a mountaintop inn served by a gondola. The architectural vocabulary of the buildings and sitework is a synthesis of northern Californian and traditional alpine vernaculars.

Physical Sciences Building, University of California, Santa Barbara
Santa Barbara, California, 1988

Slight adjustments to the plan and massing and entirely new facades were proposed for a building designed by other architects.

Columbus Retirement Community
Columbus, Indiana, 1988

This 150-unit, assisted-living retirement community was proposed for a rolling, partially wooded site on the outskirts of the architecturally notable town of Columbus, Indiana. The community's site planning, massing, and architectural imagery recall late-nineteenth-century resort hotels such as those in nearby West Baden and French Lick.

 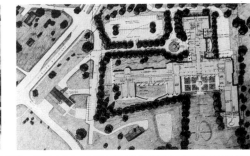

Ocean Heights
Kennebunkport, Maine, 1988

This development consists of a small house and four two-unit and one four-unit condominium and manor houses. The houses, looking across Walker Point to the sea, respect the local building traditions with gambrel roofs, bays and towers, and extensive use of stone, shingle, and painted wood.

House on Red Mountain
Aspen, Colorado, 1988

Designed as a ski house for a family that entertains frequently, this house is nestled into its site but retains a distinct presence of its own.

Mecox Fields Lot 7
Bridgehampton, New York, 1986–89

The last to be built in a coordinated enclave of six houses designed by the office, this house modifies the Shingle Style vocabulary used in the earlier houses toward a farmhouse vernacular.

 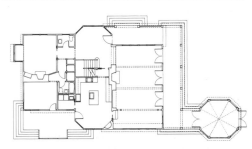

Meadowbrook II
Hempstead, New York, 1986–89

For this twenty-acre site, the site plans and building design of a typical suburban office park are interpreted through the principles and vocabulary of classicism.

 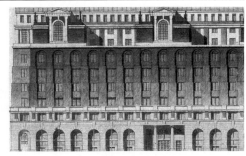

Residence at Brainard Woods
West Hartford, Connecticut, 1987–89

Designed for a developer, this house is set back on its lot to capture unobstructed views of downtown Hartford. A two-story Tuscan order brackets both front and rear facades, supporting its entablature and the gabled roof. The house is rendered in painted wood trim and trellis over naturally weathered siding, its form and detailing recalling the Connecticut rural seats of an earlier era.

Bedford Garage
Farm Neck, Martha's Vineyard, 1988–89

A propylea to the main house, which the office designed for previous owners in 1980–83.

Matanzas Shores Beach Club
Palm Coast, Florida, 1989

A small beach club inspired by the clustered groupings of Spanish farmhouses.

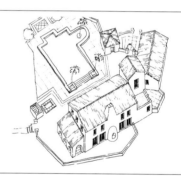

Pierson Lakes Development
Sterlington, New York, 1989

Designed to help promote a new development, this house takes its design cues from the architectural forms of the Ramapo Valley.

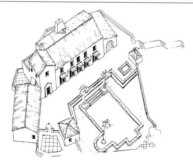

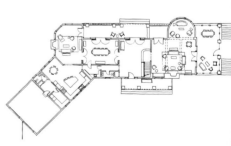

Riverwalk, Chevron Land and Development Corporation
Mission Valley, San Diego, California, 1989–

Situated in the heart of San Diego's Mission Valley, Riverwalk replaces a golf course with a new development that will include various housing neighborhoods and a 3,000,000-square-foot town center incorporating retail, hotel, office, and residential uses.

Concord Walk Hotel
Charleston, South Carolina, 1989–

A ninety-nine-room luxury inn facing the Cooper River just north of Charleston's Battery. Part of an ongoing revitalization of a historic neighborhood of now-abandoned warehouses, the hotel is made up of four individual buildings connected by bridges and facing a new waterfront park.

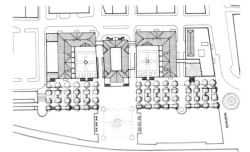 

Anglebrook Golf Club
Somers, New York, 1989–

The clubhouse is treated as a large, casually massed country house, with a picturesque mix of chimneys, gables, and dormers, stucco and half-timbered walls, columned porches, French doors, and casement windows that is typical of nearby clubs and private houses of the 1920s.

 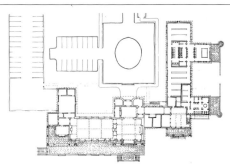

Carnegie Hill Townhouse
New York, New York, 1987–90

This design includes renovations to three floors of a townhouse and a new garden facade.

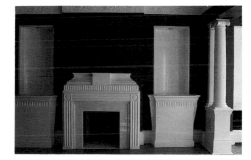 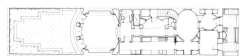

Herrmann Apartment
New York, New York, 1988–90

New architectural woodwork to complement the character of a venerable West Side apartment.

Residence at Cove Hollow Farm
East Hampton, New York, 1989–90

Replacing the original house, which was designed by the office in 1981 but was later destroyed by fire, this enlarged version elaborates, in both scale and detail, themes that were first established in its more modest antecedent.

Residence
Kiawah Island, South Carolina, 1989–90

Intended for a seventeen-acre oceanfront site, this house is designed as a series of wings and pavilions that take advantage of views and shelter formal exterior spaces.

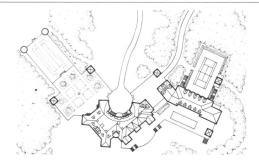

Alterations and Additions to the Edwards-Smyth House
Charleston, South Carolina, 1989–90

A proposal for modifications to the plan of a historic house and its outbuildings as well as a new swimming pool and garden.

Pool and Pergola
Kiawah Island, South Carolina, 1989–90

A latticed enclosure to provide privacy without unduly restricting the flow of breezes.

Old Merchant's House Table Ornament
1990

An ornament designed for the Preservation League of New York State's luncheon honoring Joan K. Davidson, president of the J. M. Kaplan Fund.

Disney Boardwalk Village and Hotel, Walt Disney World
Lake Buena Vista, Florida, 1990–

A hotel, shopping, and entertainment complex to be built across Lake Crescent from the firm's Yacht Club and Beach Club hotels.

The Town Square—Wheaton
Wheaton, Illinois, 1988–91

An "anchorless mall" situated in a western
suburb of Chicago, The Town Square—Wheaton
consists of approximately 160,000 square feet of
ground and mezzanine-level retail space
organized to create the sense of a traditional
village center. Two freestanding 8,000-square-
foot restaurants and an additional 85,000 square
feet of commercial development are proposed as
future phases.

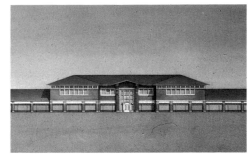

Pool and Gazebo
Kiawah Island, South Carolina, 1990–91

Inspired by traditional South Carolina forms,
this screened gazebo commands a view of the
pool and a nearby waterway.

Disney Regional Shopping Center Competition
Orlando, Florida, 1991

This proposal includes a 2,000,000-square-foot
open-to-weather regional mall as well as related
hotels and office buildings. Massed to the shape
of Florida, the mall design features a series of
villages based on regional themes and connected
by a principal street.

Residence in Beverly Park
Beverly Hills, California, 1991

Located in the hills, this residence is designed as
a compound of buildings and interrelated
landscape elements.

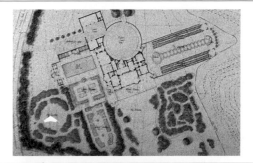

Residence in Starwood
Aspen, Colorado, 1991–

A formal stone house set atop a podium that
burrows into the hill.

Project Information

352 **Scarsdale Heights**
Scarsdale, New York, 1984

Architect-in-Charge: Graham S. Wyatt. Assistants: Barry Goralnick, Caroline Hancock.

Penthouse Apartment
New York, New York, 1984–85

Architect-in-Charge: Paul L. Whalen. Assistants: David Eastman, Caroline Hancock, William C. Nolan. Interior Design Assistants: Ingrid Armstrong, Ronne Fisher.

Elaine Markoutsas, "Home is Where the Details Are," *Baltimore Sun* (May 14, 1989), XIX: 1, 8 (U.P. syndicated column).

Carla Jean Schwartz, "The Articulate Architect," *Style* (Fall 1989): 58–63, 102.

Robert A. M. Stern Architects Office
New York, New York, 1985

Architects-in-Charge: Anthony Cohn, Thomas Nohr. Assistant: Caryl Kinsey.

"Postmodern Paradox," *Architectural Record* 175 (June 1987): 102–5.

"Architektenbüro in New York City," *Baumeister* 84 (November 1987): 46–47.

"Recent Works of Robert A. M. Stern," *Architecture and Urbanism* 212 (May 1988): 122–23.

Robert A. M. Stern: Selected Works, with an introduction by Charles Jencks (London: Academy Editions, 1991), 68–69.

Russian Hill Townhouses
San Francisco, California, 1985

Architects-in-Charge: Alan J. Gerber, Armand LeGardeur. Assistants: Warren A. James, Mark Johnson, Timothy E. Lenahan, Kristin L. McMahon, Paul Williger. Landscape Architect: Robert Ermerins. Associated Architect: Richard Hannum Associates.

Residence
Brooklyn, New York, 1983–86

Architect-in-Charge: Alan J. Gerber. Assistants: Anthony Cohn, David Eastman, William T. Georgis, Warren A. James, Kristin L. McMahon. Landscape Architect: Robert Ermerins. Interior Design Associate: Alan J. Gerber.

Luis F. Rueda, ed., *Robert A. M. Stern: Buildings and Projects 1981–1986* (New York: Rizzoli, 1986), 192–95.

Ghisi Grütter, *Il Disegno degli Architetti Americani Contemporanei* (Rome: Gangemi Editore, 1987), 134–38.

Heinrich Klotz, ed., *New York Architecture 1970–1990* (Munich: Prestel-Verlag, 1989), 220–21.

Lucia Funari, ed., *Robert A. M. Stern: Modernità e Tradizione* (Rome: Edizioni Kappa, 1990), 116–19.

Robert A. M. Stern: Selected Works, with an introduction by Charles Jencks (London: Academy Editions, 1991), 42–43.

The American Houses of Robert A. M. Stern, with an introduction by Clive Aslet (New York: Rizzoli, 1991), 202–7.

Award for Unbuilt Projects, New York Chapter, American Institute of Architects, 1985.

Executive Suite, The Druker Company
Boston, Massachusetts, 1985–86

Architect-in-Charge: John Ike. Assistants: Victoria Casasco, William C. Nolan, Dierdre O'Farrelly. Interior Design Associate: Lisa Maurer.

Mexx, USA, Inc., Fashion Showroom
New York, New York, 1985–86

Architect-in-Charge: Alexander P. Lamis, Graham S. Wyatt. Assistants: Jenny Peng, Jeff Schofield. Interior Design Assistants: Ingrid Armstrong, Tanya Kelly.

Justin Henderson, "Robert A. M. Stern Architects," *Interiors* 147 (June 1988): 154–57.

Design Excellence and Innovation, Environments Category, *ID* Annual Design Review, 1988.

Milwin Farm
Ocean Township, New Jersey, 1985–86

Architect-in-Charge: Grant Marani. Assistants: Mark Brearley, Sarah Hunnewell, Mark Johnson, Elizabeth A. Kozarec, Dierdre O'Farrelly, Constance Treadwell, Mabel O. Wilson.

"Suburban Splendor, Stern Style," *Architectural Record* 174 (November 1986): 59.

Carol Vogel, "Clustered for Leisure: The Changing Home," *New York Times Magazine* (June 28, 1987): 12–17, 38, 46, 64.

Addition to the Colonnade Hotel
Boston, Massachusetts, 1986

Architect-in-Charge: John Ike. Associated Architect: Jung/Brannen Associates, Inc.

Craftsman Farms
Parsippany, New Jersey, 1986

Architect-in-Charge: Anthony Cohn. Project Associate: Keller A. Easterling.

Patricia Herold, "A Stickley Business," *Metropolitan Home* 20 (February 1988): 22.

Patricia Herold, "Town, Stickley Buffs to Save Craftsman Farms," *Preservation News* 29 (May 1989): 1, 6.

Carol A. Crotta, "Stickley Saved," *Home* 35 (November 1989): 14.

"Preservation: Stickley's Craftsman Farms," *Progressive Architecture* 71 (June 1990): 26.

Residence
Wassenaar, The Netherlands, 1986

Project Architect: Graham S. Wyatt. Assistants: Preston J. Gumberich, Jeff Schofield, Paul B. Williger. Local Architect: Henk van de Meent Architects.

Leen van Duin, "Mexx in Voorschoten," *Architectonische Studies* 5 (Delft: Delftse Universitaire Pers, 1988), 9–31.

Leen van Duin, Willemijn Wilms Floet, "Soms Is Iets Zo Mooi Dat Het Herhaald Moet Worden," *Archis* (February 1988): 44–51.

Desert House
Phoenix, Arizona, 1986

Architect-in-Charge: William T. Georgis. Landscape Architect: Robert Ermerins.

Ettl Farm Development
Princeton, New Jersey, 1986

Architect-in-Charge: Alexander P. Lamis. Assistant: Preston J. Gumberich.

Apartment House, Fan Pier Development
Boston, Massachusetts, 1986

Architect-in-Charge: John Ike. Project Associate: Timothy E. Lenahan. Assistants: Augusta Barone, Ellen Kenyon Coxe, Keller A. Easterling, William T. Georgis, Mark Johnson. Master Plan Architect: Cesar Pelli Associates. Production/Coordinating Architect: Steffian Bradley.

Roy Strickland, "No Little Plans: An Ambitious Mixed-Use Scheme for Boston," *Architectural Record* 175 (February 1987): 60–61.

Jane Holtz Kay, "New Design for Boston Piers," *Progressive Architecture* 68 (April 1987): 35–36.

"A Tale of Two (or More) Cities," *Metropolis* 6 (June 1987): 18–22.

Paul Goldberger, "Boston's Chance for its Own Battery Park City," *New York Times* (June 28, 1987), II: 25.

Jonathan Barnett, "In the Public Interest: Design Guidelines," *Architectural Record* 175 (July 1987): 114–25.

Giancarlo Priori, "Ritrovare i Propri Dèi," *Eupalino* 9/10 (1988): 31–36.

Lucia Funari, ed., *Robert A. M. Stern: Modernità e Tradizione* (Rome: Edizioni Kappa, 1990), 186–89.

"Fan Pier Master Plan, Boston, Massachusetts," *Architecture and Urbanism* 233 (February 1990): 144–48.

Pershing Square Competition
Los Angeles, California, 1986

Architect-in-Charge: Charles D. Warren. Associated Architects: Michael C. F. Chan and Associates, Inc.

"Winner Selected for Pershing Square," *Progressive Architecture* 67 (September 1986): 23–24.

"A Conversation," *Landscape Architecture* 77 (January/February 1987): 90–95.

Lucia Funari, ed., *Robert A. M. Stern: Modernità e Tradizione* (Rome: Edizioni Kappa, 1990), 190–91.

Essex Bay Estates
West Gloucester, Massachusetts, 1986

Architect-in-Charge: Joseph W. Dick. Assistants: Dierdre O'Farrelly, Jay A. Waronker.

Kiluna Farms
North Hills, New York, 1986

Architect-in-Charge: Anthony Cohn. Assistants: Karen E. Small, Pat Tiné, Paul B. Williger.

Swid Powell Series II
1986

Architect-in-Charge: William T. Georgis. Assistant: Silvina Geofron.

Carol Vogel, "Currents: He's Got Designs on These Plates," *New York Times* (January 14, 1988), III: 3.

Michael Collins and Andreas Papadakis, *Post-Modern Design* (New York: Rizzoli, 1989), 131–32, 158–59.

Annette Tapert, *Swid Powell: Objects by Architects* (New York: Rizzoli, 1990), 96–105.

Suzanne Slesin, "Architects Show How to Set a Grand Table," *New York Times* (November 29, 1990), III: 6.

"Last-Minute Gifts," *W* (December 10–17, 1990): 65.

"Design News: For the (Very) Well-Dressed Table," *Architectural Record* 179 (January 1991): 25.

Mitchell Owens, "Au Courant," *Elle Decor* 2 (April 1991): 22.

Brent C. Brolin, "At Swid Powell, the Architects' Collection of Tableware," *New York Observer* 5 (May 13, 1991): 20.

Apartment Tower, Union Theological Seminary
Claremont Tower, Manhattan School of Music
New York, New York, 1986, 1987

Architect-in-Charge: John Ike. Assistants: Ellen Kenyon Coxe, Thomas M. Eisele, Timothy E. Lenahan.

Two Newton Place
Newton, Massachusetts, 1984–87

Architect-in-Charge: John Ike. Assistants: Victoria Casasco, Alexander P. Lamis, Jeff Schofield, Graham S. Wyatt. Associated Architect: Drummey Rosane Anderson, Inc.

John Arthur, "Alternative Space: Robert A. M. Stern," *Art New England* 6 (April 1985): 8–9.

Luis F. Rueda, ed., *Robert A. M. Stern: Buildings and Projects 1981–1986* (New York: Rizzoli, 1986), 212–15.

"Stern, SOM Designs Highlight Newton Center," *Building Design Journal* 4 (January 1986): 6.

Eric Stange, "Brave New Boston," *Boston Herald Magazine* (February 16, 1986): 4–7.

"Redefining the Low-Rise Office Building: Two Current Projects by Robert A. M. Stern," *Architectural Record* 174 (March 1986): 53.

Residence
Marblehead, Massachusetts, 1984–87

Architect-in-Charge: Roger H. Seifter. Senior Assistant: Caroline Hancock. Assistant: Kaarin Taipale.

Luis F. Rueda, ed., *Robert A. M. Stern: Buildings and Projects 1981–1986* (New York: Rizzoli, 1986), 250–51.

Robert A. M. Stern, "Design as Emulation," in Dr. Andreas C. Papadakis, ed., *Imitation and Innovation* (London: Architectural Design, 1988): 20–24, 26–27.

Mark Muro, "The Architect as Superman," *Boston Globe* (February 5, 1988): 69–70.

"Recent Works of Robert A. M. Stern," *Architecture and Urbanism* 212 (May 1988): 120–21.

Carla Jean Schwartz, "The Articulate Architect," *Style* (Fall 1989): 58–62, 102.

Lucia Funari, ed., *Robert A. M. Stern: Modernità e Tradizione* (Rome: Edizioni Kappa, 1990), 126–33.

Elaine Markoutsas, "Architecturally Speaking," *San Jose Mercury News* (June 30, 1990), V: 1, 4.

Robert A. M. Stern: Selected Works, with an introduction by Charles Jencks (London: Academy Editions, 1991), 62–65, 112.

The American Houses of Robert A. M. Stern, with an introduction by Clive Aslet (New York: Rizzoli, 1991), 120–25.

354 **Sunstone**
Quogue, New York, 1984–87

Architect-in-Charge: Randy M. Correll. Assistants: Thomas Nohr, Constance Treadwell.

Luis F. Rueda, ed., *Robert A. M. Stern: Buildings and Projects 1981–1986* (New York: Rizzoli, 1986), 198.

Carol Vogel, "The Home Team," *New York Times Magazine* (August 5, 1990): 54–59.

Robert A. M. Stern: Selected Works, with an introduction by Charles Jencks (London: Academy Editions, 1991), 68–69.

The American Houses of Robert A. M. Stern, with an introduction by Clive Aslet (New York: Rizzoli, 1991), 126–35.

Residence at Calf Creek
Water Mill, New York, 1984–87

Architect-in-Charge: Armand LeGardeur. Assistant: Luis F. Rueda-Salazar. Landscape Architect: Robert Ermerins. Interior Design Associate: Lisa Maurer.

Luis F. Rueda, ed., *Robert A. M. Stern: Buildings and Projects 1981–1986* (New York: Rizzoli, 1986), 198–99.

Clive Aslet, "Stern by Name, Not Nature," *Country Life* 180 (October 30, 1986): 1354–56.

Kurt Andersen, "Robert A. M. Stern: New Interpretation of the Shingle Style on Long Island," *Architectural Digest* 46 (August 1989): 66–71, 94, 98.

Robert A. M. Stern: Selected Works, with an introduction by Charles Jencks (London: Academy Editions, 1991), 56–59.

The American Houses of Robert A. M. Stern, with an introduction by Clive Aslet (New York: Rizzoli, 1991), 136–45.

Citation, Long Island Chapter, American Institute of Architects, 1988; Excellence in Design Award, New York State Association of Architecture, American Institute of Architects, 1989.

The Hamptons
Lexington, Massachusetts, 1985–87

Architects-in-Charge: Thomas P. Catalano, Joseph W. Dick, John Ike. Assistants: Anthony Cohn, Natalie Jacobs, Graham S. Wyatt.

Luis F. Rueda, ed., *Robert A. M. Stern: Buildings and Projects 1981–1986* (New York: Rizzoli, 1986), 280–83.

Marion J. Costen, "Victorian Revisited," *Boston Herald* (April 17, 1986): 41, 46.

Sharon Lee Ryder, "On the Right Tract: The New Suburban Dream House," *Metropolitan Home* 18 (November 1986): 39.

Penelope Lemov, "Marketing by Design," *Builder* 10 (August 1987): 54–59.

Robert Campbell, "Stern's Fresh Approach to the Shingle Style," *Boston Globe* (January 5, 1988): 66.

Mary McLeod, "Architecture and Politics in the Reagan Era: From Postmodernism to Deconstructivism," *Assemblage* 8 (February 1989): 23–59.

Isabel Forgang, "Grand Entrances," *Elle Decor* 1 (Winter 1990): 74–76.

International Headquarters, Mexx International, B.V.
Voorschoten, The Netherlands, 1985–87

Architect-in-Charge: Graham S. Wyatt. Assistants: Preston J. Gumberich, Grant Marani, William C. Nolan, Jenny Peng, Jeff Schofield, Pat Tiné. Landscape Architect: Robert Ermerins. Local Architect: Henk van de Meent Architects.

Stanley Tigerman, ed., *The Chicago Tapes* (New York: Rizzoli, 1987), 10–19.

Carla Debets, "Een Kantoorgebouw met Twee Gezichten," *Bouw Wereld* 83 (June 26, 1987): 26–29.

Leen van Duin, "Mexx in Voorschoten," "Interview met Robert Stern," "Interview met Graham Wyatt," "Interview met Henk van de Meent," W. Wilms Floet, "Plandocumentatie Mexx Voorschooten," *Architectonische Studies* 5 (Delft: Delftse Universitaire Pers, 1988): 9–65.

Andreas C. Papadakis, *Contemporary Architecture* (London: Architectural Design, 1988): 71–75.

Leen van Duin, Willemijn Wilms Floet, "Soms Is Iets Zo Mooi Dat Het Herhaald Moet Worden," *Archis* (February 1988): 44–51.

Deborah K. Dietsch, "Time Warp," *Architectural Record* 176 (May 1988): 106–13.

"Recent Works of Robert A. M. Stern," *Architecture and Urbanism* 212 (May 1988): 64–83.

"Verwaltungsbau in Voorschoten," *Baumeister* 85 (August 1988): 32–38.

Giancarlo Priori, "Robert Stern: Ritrovare i Propri Dèi," *Eupalino* 9/10 (1988): 31–36.

Heinrich Klotz, ed., *New York Architecture 1970–1990* (Munich: Prestel-Verlag, 1989), 318–19.

Lucia Funari, ed., *Robert A. M. Stern: Modernità e Tradizione* (Rome: Edizioni Kappa, 1990), 152–55.

Monica Zerboni, "Lo Stile Si Fa In Tre," *Construire* 85 (June 1990): 201–4.

Marc Bédarida and Milka Milatovic, *Immeubles de Bureaux* (Paris: Edition du Moniteur, 1991), 109.

Robert A. M. Stern: Selected Works, with an introduction by Charles Jencks (London: Academy Editions, 1991), 70–75, 119, 124, 129.

National Honor Award, American Institute of Architects, 1990.

Residence at Taylor's Creek
Southampton, New York, 1985–87

Architect-in-Charge: Armand LeGardeur. Assistant: Elizabeth A. Kozarec. Landscape Architect: Robert Ermerins.

Mexx Retail Shop
150 Peter Cornelius Hoofstraat, Amsterdam, The Netherlands, 1986–87

Architects-in-Charge: Alexander P. Lamis, Graham S. Wyatt. Assistants: Jeff Schofield, Pat Tiné. Associated Architect: Dik Smeding, Architectburo.

Hans Ibelings, "Robert Stern Bouwt in Voorschoten en Amsterdam," *Archis* (July 1987): 6.

Leen van Duin, "Mexx in Voorschoten," *Architectonische Studies* 5 (Delft: Delftse Universitaire Pers, 1988): 9–65.

Tracy Metz, "The Mirror of Fashion," *Architectural Record* 176 (May 1988): 138–41.

Toshio Nakamura, "Recent Works of Robert A. M. Stern," *Architecture and Urbanism* 212 (May 1988): 84–95.

Heinrich Klotz, ed., *New York Architecture 1970–1990* (Munich: Prestel-Verlag, 1989), 318.

Upper East Side Apartment
New York, New York, 1986–87

Architect-in-Charge: Armand LeGardeur. Assistant: Elizabeth A. Kozarec.

Wendy W. Staebler, *Architectural Detailing in Residential Interiors* (New York: Whitney Library of Design, 1990), 174–75.

Winchester Country Club
Winchester, Virginia, 1987

Architect-in-Charge: Stephen T. B. Falatko. Assistants: Mary Cerrone, William T. Georgis, Timothy E. Lenahan, Derrick W. Smith.

Townhouse Apartment
New York, New York, 1987

Architect-in-Charge: Alan J. Gerber. Project Associate: Elizabeth Thompson.

An Owligorical House (Otus Asio)
1987

Architect-in-Charge: William T. Georgis. Assistant: Mark Johnson.

Patricia Leigh Brown, "53 Architects Design for the Fine Feathered Set," *New York Times* (May 21, 1987), III: 1, 6.

Lynn Nesmith, "Birdhouses Designed by Architects," *Architecture* 76 (July 1987): 29.

Heather Smith MacIsaac and Senga Mortimer, "Architecture for the Birds," *House & Garden* 159 (July 1987): 106–9.

Barry Bergdoll, "Bird Houses by Architects," *Progressive Architecture* 68 (July 1987): 27.

Toshio Nakamura, "Recent Works of Robert A. M. Stern," *Architecture and Urbanism* 212 (May 1988): 124.

Leslie Garisto, *From Bauhaus to Birdhouse* (New York: Harper Collins, 1992), frontispiece, 53.

Sailors' Snug Harbor Music Halls Competition
Staten Island, New York, 1987

Architect-in-Charge: Stephen T. B. Falatko. Assistants: Augusta Barone, Mary Cerrone, John S. Mason. Associated Architect: Robert E. Meadows, P.C. Architects.

Paul Goldberger, "The Slow, Stylish Redesign of Snug Harbor," *New York Times* (July 5, 1987), II: 24.

"The Snug Harbor Music Hall Competition," *Oculus* (September 1987): 4–7, 14–19.

The Grace Estate
East Hampton, New York, 1987

Architect-in-Charge: Randy M. Correll. Assistants: Joseph W. Dick, Yvonne Galindo, Abigail M. Huffman, Daniel Romualdez, Lisa Rothkrug, Karen E. Small, Jay A. Waronker. Landscape Architect: Robert Ermerins. Landscape Assistant: William C. Skelsey.

Diana Shaman, "Waterfront Project in East Hampton," *New York Times* (March 3, 1989): 28.

Richmond Visitors' Center Competition
Richmond, Virginia, 1987

Architect-in-Charge: Stephen T. B. Falatko. Assistants: John S. Mason, Jay

A. Waronker. Associated Architect: Marcellus Wright Cox & Smith, Architects.

Tom Campbell, "Two Agencies Choose Classic Style for Center," *Richmond Times-Dispatch* (September 9, 1987), II: 5.

Lucia Funari, ed., *Robert A. M. Stern: Modernità e Tradizione* (Rome: Edizioni Kappa, 1990), 200–201.

Santa Agueda Resort, Gran Canaria
Canary Islands, Spain, 1987

Architect-in-Charge: Paul L. Whalen. Assistants: Sonia R. Cháo, Warren A. James, Timothy E. Lenahan, Daniel Lobitz.

Akademie der Wissenschaften Competition
Berlin, Germany, 1987

Architect-in-Charge: William T. Georgis. Assistant: Silvina Goefron. Renderers: David J. Dwight, William T. Georgis, Silvina Goefron, James Herman, Liza Phillips, Andrew Zega.

Dr. Andreas C. Papadakis, ed., *Imitation and Innovation* (London: Architectural Design, 1988): 20–24.

Robert A. M. Stern, "Akademie der Wissenschaften Competition," *Oz: Journal of the College of Architecture and Design, Kansas State University* 10 (1988): 20–21.

Toshio Nakamura, ed., "Recent Works of Robert A. M. Stern," *Architecture and Urbanism* 212 (May 1988): 140–41.

Mary Pepchinski, "Berlin Academy of Science Competition and Controversy," *Progressive Architecture* 69 (June 1988): 27, 29–30.

Pigeon Cove
Rockport, Massachusetts, 1987

Architect-in-Charge: Grant Marani. Assistants: Mark Brearley, Mark Johnson, Luis F. Rueda-Salazar, Mabel O. Wilson.

42nd Street Theaters
New York, New York, 1987

Architect-in-Charge: Stephen T. B. Falatko. Assistants: Austin Brown, Philip Brown, Alexis O. Fernandez, David Fishman, Luis Fontcuberta, Sharon Pett, Lisa Rothkrug, Andrew Zega.

Carter B. Horsley, "Site Switch in Times Square Plan," *New York Post* (August 21, 1987): 16.

David W. Dunlap, "Agency Acts to Speed Times Sq. Project," *New York Times* (August 21, 1987), II: 3.

"Follow Up," *New York Landmarks Conservancy Newsletter* 5 (Fall/Winter 1988), unpaginated.

"'Populist' Plans for 42nd Street," *Progressive Architecture* 69 (November 1988): 24, 28.

Paul Goldberger, "Lack of Money Threatens a Plan To Restore Six Times Sq. Theaters," *New York Times* (November 14, 1988), I: 1, II: 2.

"42nd Street: No Beat of Dancing Feet—Yet," *Architectural Record* 177 (June 1989): 85.

"New Revivals for Times Square," *Oculus* 52 (October 1989): 9.

New Town
Orlando, Florida, 1987

Architect-in-Charge: Paul L. Whalen. Project Associates: Keller A. Easterling, Alexander P. Lamis. Assistants: David J. Dwight, Gordon Trachtenberg.

356   **Frankfurt Jewish Memorial Competition**
Frankfurt, Germany, 1987

Architect-in-Charge: William T. Georgis. Assistants: Bernd Dams, Robert Kennett, Andrew Zega.

Residence
Winnetka, Illinois, 1987

Architect-in-Charge: Roger H. Seifter. Assistant: Olivia Rowan.

Cap d'Akiya
Hayama, Japan, 1987–

Architect-in-Charge: Grant Marani. Assistants: Thomas M. Eisele, W. David Henderson, Caryl Kinsey, Luis F. Rueda-Salazar, Lynn H. Wang, Mabel O. Wilson, Rosamund Young. Associated Architect: Kajima Corporation.

Toshio Nakamura, "Recent Works of Robert A. M. Stern," *Architecture and Urbanism* 212 (May 1988): 142–43.

"Robert A. M. Stern," *Nikkei Architecture* 324 (August 1988): 202–5.

"In Progress," *Progressive Architecture* 69 (November 1988): 42.

Nora Richter Greer, "Americans Abroad: Some Coming Attractions," *Architecture* 78 (January 1989): 64–71.

Naomi R. Pollack, "Foreign Architects are Building Bridges to Japan," *New York Times* (March 8, 1992), II: 36.

Patricof Apartment
New York, New York, 1982, 1986–88

Architect-in-Charge: Alan J. Gerber. Assistants: Mary Cerrone, Kenneth McIntyre-Horito.

Residence at Lily Pond Lane
East Hampton, New York, 1983–85, 1988

Architect-in-Charge: Randy M. Correll. Landscape Architect: Robert Ermerins. Landscape Assistant: William C. Skelsey. Interior Design Associate: Randy M. Correll.

Luis F. Rueda, ed., *Robert A. M. Stern: Buildings and Projects 1981–1986* (New York: Rizzoli, 1986), 232–33.

Vincent Scully, "Robert A. M. Stern: New Spaces in an East Hampton Shingle-Style Cottage," *Architectural Digest* 44 (September 1987): 26–31.

Excellence in Design, New York State Association of Architects, American Institute of Architects, 1988.

Residence
Hewlett Harbor, New York, 1984–88

Architect-in-Charge: Charles D. Warren. Assistants: Re Hagele, Grant Marani, Jenny Peng, Elizabeth Thompson. Landscape Architect: Robert Ermerins. Interior Design Associate: Lisa Maurer.

Luis F. Rueda, ed., *Robert A. M. Stern: Buildings and Projects 1981–1986* (New York: Rizzoli, 1986), 190–91.

Deborah A. Kunstler, "Elegance that Entertains," *Newsday* (February 23, 1986): 30–33.

Robert A. M. Stern: Selected Works, with an introduction by Charles Jencks (London: Academy Editions, 1991), 66–67, 120, 123.

The American Houses of Robert A. M. Stern, with an introduction by Clive Aslet (New York: Rizzoli, 1991), 110–19.

Alterations and Additions to the Sunningdale Country Club
Scarsdale, New York, 1985–88

Architect-in-Charge: Anthony Cohn. Project Associate: Keller A. Easterling. Assistant: Warren A. James.

Middlesea Residence
East Hampton, New York, 1985–88

Architect-in-Charge: Roger H. Seifter. Senior Assistant: Diane J. Smith. Assistants: Richard Economakis, Yvonne Galindo. Landscape Architect: Robert Ermerins. Landscape Assistants: Holly Nelson, Patrick Santana.

The Shops at Somerset Square
Glastonbury, Connecticut, 1986–88

Architect-in-Charge: Graham S. Wyatt. Senior Assistant: Jeff Schofield. Assistants: Preston J. Gumberich, William C. Nolan, Pat Tiné, Gary Tschirhart.

Eleanor Charles, "Town Square Reborn in Shopping Center," *New York Times* (May 8, 1988), X: 10.

Giancarlo Priori, "Ritrovare i Propri Dèi," *Eupalino* 9/10 (1988): 31–36.

Daralice D. Boles, "Reordering the Suburbs," *Progressive Architecture* 70 (May 1989): 78–91.

Lucia Funari, ed., *Robert A. M. Stern: Modernità e Tradizione* (Rome: Edizioni Kappa, 1990), 164–67.

Merit Award, International Council of Shopping Centers Annual Design Awards, 1988; Merit Award, *Builder,* 1989.

Renovations to a Residence in Edgartown
Martha's Vineyard, Massachusetts, 1986–88

Architects-in-Charge: Joseph W. Dick, Paul L. Whalen. Assistant: Dierdre O'Farrelly.

Residence on Prospect Avenue
Hartford, Connecticut, 1986–88

Architect-in-Charge: Joseph W. Dick. Assistants: Dierdre O'Farrelly, Jeff Schofield, Jay A. Waronker.

Wynnewood Houses
Stamford, Connecticut, 1986–88

Architect-in-Charge: Grant Marani. Assistants: Adam Anuszkiewicz, Sarah Hunnewell, Mark Johnson, Elizabeth A. Kozarec, Luis F. Rueda-Salazar, Mabel O. Wilson.

Mark McCain, "Building Million-Dollar Mansions, On Spec," *New York Times* (February 5, 1989), X: 1, 18.

Maggie Malone and Cathleen McGuigan, "High Style in the 'Burbs," *Newsweek* 113 (March 27, 1989): 64–66.

Eleanor Charles, "If You're Thinking of Living in: Stamford," *New York Times* (August 20, 1989), X: 5.

Decorative Arts for Munari Associati
1987–88

Architect-in-Charge: William T. Georgis. Assistant: Silvina Goefron.

Michael Collins and Andreas Papadakis, *Post-Modern Design* (New York: Rizzoli, 1989), 131, 132, 160.

Susan Jones and Marilyn Nissenson, *Cuff Links* (New York: Harry N. Abrams, 1991), 105.

California Lifeguard Tower
1988

Architect-in-Charge: William T. Georgis. Assistant: Silvina Goefron.

"Kalifornien: Neue Turme fur den Strand," *Häuser* 4 (1988): 11.

Patricia Leigh Brown, "Cowabunga! Lifeguard Towers as Art," *New York Times* (July 14, 1988), III: 1, 12.

Terry Bissel, "Kowabunga," *Main* 3 (September/October/November 1988): unpaginated.

"'California Lifeguard Towers' at Kirsten Kiser Gallery," *Architecture and Urbanism* 217 (October 1988): 10.

Victoria Geibel, "On the Beach," *Metropolis* 8 (October 1988): 63.

Huppah for Temple Emanu-El
New York, New York, 1988

Architect-in-Charge: William T. Georgis. Assistant: Silvina Goefron.

Bergdorf Goodman Window
New York, New York, 1988

Architect-in-Charge: William T. Georgis. Assistant: Silvina Goefron.

Elaine Louie, "Currents: Homely Windows," *New York Times* (January 28, 1988), III: 3.

Carol Vogel, "Currents: High-Style Windows," *New York Times* (May 5, 1988), III: 1, 30.

James Reginato, "Windows by Design," *7 Days* 1 (May 11, 1988): 24.

Paul Goldberger, "Shows Celebrate New York Architecture," *New York Times* (May 13, 1988), III: 1, 24.

Charles Gandee, "Window Dressing," *House & Garden* 160 (June 1988): 29.

"A Photo Album From the Convention," *Oculus* 50 (June 1988): 7.

Karen D. Stein, "Bergdorf Goodman Fifth Avenue Windows, New York City," *Architectural Record* 176 (July 1988): 96–97.

"AIA/NY: Window Shopping," *Progressive Architecture* 69 (July 1988): 23.

Edie Lee Cohen, "Bergdorf Goodman Salutes the AIA," *Interior Design* 59 (September 1988): 264–65.

Laurel Harper, "On Display: Architectonics," *VM & SD* 119 (October 1988): 40–45.

Annette Tapert, *Swid Powell: Objects by Architects* (New York: Rizzoli, 1990), 32–33.

Centro Cultural de Belem Competition
Lisbon, Portugal, 1988

Architect-in-Charge: William T. Georgis. Senior Assistant: Lee Ledbetter. Assistants: Silvina Goefron, E. J. Jarboe, Anthony Poon, Ken Van Kesteren, Andrew Zega.

South Pointe Court Competition
Miami Beach, Florida, 1988

Architect-in-Charge: Paul L. Whalen. Assistants: John Berson, Christopher Blake, Laurie D. Kerr, Anthony Poon.

Master Plan and Design, Colleges 9 and 10, University of California, Santa Cruz
Santa Cruz, California, 1988

Architect-in-Charge: Graham S. Wyatt. Senior Assistant: Sandra L. Parsons.

Assistant: Paul Thompson. Landscape Architect: Robert Ermerins. Landscape Assistant: William C. Skelsey. Associated Architect: Gordon H. Chong & Associates.

Arrowwood Village
Ryebrook, New York, 1988

Architect-in-Charge: Grant Marani. Assistant: Lee Ledbetter.

Squaw Valley Master Plan and High Camp Ski Lodge
Squaw Valley, California, 1988

Architects-in-Charge, Master Plan: Graham S. Wyatt, Paul L. Whalen. Architect-in-Charge, High Camp: Graham S. Wyatt. Senior Assistant, High Camp: Preston J. Gumberich. Assistant, High Camp: Peter Himmelstein. Assistants, Master Plan: Preston J. Gumberich, Irene Hagle, Warren A. James, Lee Ledbetter, Sandra L. Parsons, Sharon Pett, Maria Resende, Ken Van Kesteren, Michael White.

Physical Sciences Building, University of California, Santa Barbara
Santa Barbara, California, 1988

Architect-in-Charge: Graham S. Wyatt. Assistant: Lee Ledbetter.

Nittsu Fujimi Land Golf Club
Izu Peninsula, Japan, 1988

Architect-in-Charge: Grant Marani. Senior Assistant: Lee Ledbetter. Assistant: Thomas Gay. Associated Architect: Kajima Corporation.

Joseph Giovannini, "Go East Young Architect," *House & Garden* 162 (February 1990): 40–42.

Harborview
Baltimore, Maryland, 1988

Architect-in-Charge: Paul L. Whalen. Project Associate: Thomas M. Eisele. Assistants: Christopher Blake, Timothy Haines, Laurie D. Kerr, Daniel Lobitz.

Columbus Retirement Community
Columbus, Indiana, 1988

Architect-in-Charge: Graham S. Wyatt. Assistant: Preston J. Gumberich.

Ocean Heights
Kennebunkport, Maine, 1988

Architect-in-Charge: Grant Marani. Assistant: Lee Ledbetter.

Laurie Ledgard, "Streamlined Langford Project Reviewed," *York County Coast Star* (October 4, 1989), I: 17–18.

House on Red Mountain
Aspen, Colorado, 1988

Architect-in-Charge: Armand LeGardeur. Assistants: Rosamund Young, Derrick W. Smith. Landscape Architect: Robert Ermerins. Landscape Assistant: William C. Skelsey.

First Government House Competition
Sydney, Australia, 1988

Architects-in-Charge: Grant Marani, Barry Rice. Assistants: Michael D. Jones, Lee Ledbetter, Andrew Zega.

Residence in North York
Ontario, Canada, 1988–

Architect-in-Charge: Roger H. Seifter. Project Associate: Kristin L. McMahon. Senior Assistant: Diane J. Smith. Assistants: Abigail M.

358 Huffman, Olivia Rowan. Landscape Architect: Robert Ermerins. Landscape Assistant: Charlotte M. Frieze. Associated Architect: Gabor + Popper Architects Inc.

The American Houses of Robert A. M. Stern, with an introduction by Clive Aslet (New York: Rizzoli, 1991), 216–19.

Copperflagg Corporation Residential Development
Staten Island, New York, 1983–89

Architect-in-Charge: Stephen T. B. Falatko. Assistants: Mary Cerrone, Keller A. Easterling, Robert Ermerins, William T. Georgis, Sarah Hunnewell, Natalie Jacobs, Warren A. James, Alexander P. Lamis, William J. LeBlanc, Richard Manion, John S. Mason, John M. Massengale, Kristin L. McMahon, Thai Nguyen, Dierdre O'Farrelly, Eric Schiller, Roger H. Seifter, Constance Treadwell, Charles D. Warren, Paul L. Whalen, Graham S. Wyatt.

Stan Pinkwas, "Leaps of Faith," *Metropolis* 3 (October 1983): 13–17, 30.

"Projects Portfolio: Robert A. M. Stern Architects," *Progressive Architecture* 64 (December 1983): 29–30, 34.

Carol Vogel, "The Trend-Setting Traditionalism of Robert A. M. Stern," *New York Times Magazine* (January 13, 1985): 40–43, 46–49.

Susan Zevon, "Building the American Dream," *House Beautiful* 127 (November 1985): 70–75.

Luis F. Rueda, ed., *Robert A. M. Stern: Buildings and Projects 1981–1986* (New York: Rizzoli, 1986), 174–83.

"Robert Stern und der Moderne Traditionalism," *Baumeister* 83 (July 1986): 44–61.

Daralice D. Boles, "P/A Profile: Suburban Stern," *Progressive Architecture* 67 (August 1986): 68–79.

"File of Architect: Robert A. M. Stern Architects," *AT Architecture* (November 1988): 32–33.

Villa in New Jersey
1983–89

Architect-in-Charge: Thomas A. Kligerman. Assistants: Augusta Barone, Victoria Casasco, Arthur D. Chabon, Bernd Dams, William T. Georgis, Natalie Jacobs, Laurie Kerr, Françoise Sogno. Landscape Architect: Robert Ermerins. Interior Design Assistants: Ingrid Armstrong, Stephan Johnson, Tanya Kelly, Lisa Maurer.

Luis F. Rueda, ed., *Robert A. M. Stern: Buildings and Projects 1981–1986* (New York: Rizzoli, 1986), 150–53.

Clive Aslet, "Stern by Name, Not Nature," *Country Life* 180 (October 30, 1986): 1354–56.

Giancarlo Priori, "Robert Stern: Ritrovare i Propri Dèi," *Eupalino* 9/10 (1988): 31–36.

Robert A. M. Stern, *Modern Classicism* (New York: Rizzoli, 1988), 224, 227.

"File of Architect: Robert A. M. Stern Architects, 1983–1987," *AT Architecture* (November 1988): 22–23.

Robert Campbell, "Remaking the Mediterranean Style," *Architectural Digest* 47 (December 1990): 102–11.

Robert A. M. Stern: Selected Works, with an introduction by Charles Jencks (London: Academy Editions, 1991), 50–55.

The American Houses of Robert A. M. Stern, with an introduction by Clive Aslet (New York: Rizzoli, 1991), 170–89.

Award for Unbuilt Projects, New York Chapter, American Institute of Architects, 1985.

Tegeler Hafen
Berlin, Germany, 1985–89

Architect-in-Charge: Graham S. Wyatt. Assistants: Ellen Kenyon Coxe, Paul B. Williger. Local Architect: Hahndle, Wolf und Zell Architektenburo, GMBH. Consulting Architect: Moritz Muller. Master Plan Architect: Moore, Ruble, Yudell Architects.

Luis F. Rueda, ed., *Robert A. M. Stern: Buildings and Projects 1981–1986* (New York: Rizzoli, 1986), 262–63.

Project Report (Berlin: Internationale Bauausstellung, 1987), 16–19.

Kurt Andersen, "Rebuilding Berlin—Yet Again," *Time* 129 (June 15, 1987): 66–68.

Joseph Giovannini, "Changing the Face of West Berlin," *New York Times* (April 14, 1988), III: 1, 12.

Deborah K. Dietsch, "Americans in Berlin—Tegel Harbor," *Architectural Record* 177 (July 1989): 82–89.

Peter Rumpf, "Less or Moore," *Bauwelt* 80 (July 1989): 1342–53.

Falk Jaeger, "Lernen von der IBA," *Baumeister* 86 (December 1989): 20–23, 36–39.

Lucia Funari, ed., *Robert A. M. Stern: Modernità e Tradizione* (Rome: Edizioni Kappa, 1990), 134–35.

Julie V. Iovine, "Socially Aware Isn't Square," *Metropolitan Home* 21 (May 1990): 77, 166.

Robert A. M. Stern: Selected Works, with an introduction by Charles Jencks (London: Academy Editions, 1991), 80–83, 108.

Residence
Pottersville, New Jersey, 1985–89

Architect-in-Charge: Randy M. Correll. Assistants: Dierdre O'Farrelly, Olivia Rowan. Interior Design Associate: Randy M. Correll.

Luis F. Rueda, ed., *Robert A. M. Stern: Buildings and Projects 1981–1986* (New York: Rizzoli, 1986), 254.

The American Houses of Robert A. M. Stern, with an introduction by Clive Aslet (New York: Rizzoli, 1991), 48–55.

Steven M.L. Aronson, "Architecture: Robert A. M. Stern; Shingle Traditions Transported to the New Jersey Hunting Country," *Architectural Digest* 48 (December 1991): 134–39.

Kol Israel Synagogue
3211 Bedford House, Brooklyn, New York, 1985–89

Architect-in-Charge: Thomas A. Kligerman. Project Associates: Caryl Kinsey, Laurie D. Kerr. Assistants: Augusta Barone, Victoria Casasco, Peter Dick, Michelle Huot, Timothy E. Lenahan, Jeffrey Wilkinson.

Luis F. Rueda, ed., *Robert A. M. Stern: Buildings and Projects 1981–1986* (New York: Rizzoli, 1986), 266–67.

"A Synagogue Grows in Brooklyn," *Architectural Record* 175 (June 1987): 55.

"File of Architect: Robert A. M. Stern Architects, 1983–1987," *AT Architecture* (November 1988): 27.

Heinrich Klotz, ed., *New York Architecture 1970–1990* (Munich: Prestel-Verlag, 1989), 222–23.

Lucia Funari, ed., *Robert A. M. Stern: Modernità e Tradizione* (Rome: Edizioni Kappa, 1990), 142–45.

Robert A. M. Stern: Selected Works, with an introduction by Charles Jencks (London: Academy Editions, 1991), 76–77.

Residence on Russian Hill
San Francisco, California, 1985–89

Architect-in-Charge: Alan J. Gerber. Project Associates: Kristin L. McMahon, Elizabeth Thompson. Assistants: Kenneth McIntyre-Horito, Warren A. James. Associated Architect: Richard Hannum Associates.

Luis F. Rueda, ed., *Robert A. M. Stern: Buildings and Projects 1981–1986* (New York: Rizzoli, 1986), 275.

Paul Goldberger, "Architecture: Robert A. M. Stern," *Architectural Digest* 47 (October 1990): 196–205.

Sally Woodbridge, "Rising to the Occasion," *Progressive Architecture* 71 (November 1990): 80–85.

Robert A. M. Stern: Selected Works, with an introduction by Charles Jencks (London: Academy Editions, 1991), 78–79, 111.

The American Houses of Robert A. M. Stern, with an introduction by Clive Aslet (New York: Rizzoli, 1991), 208–15.

Residence
Elberon, New Jersey, 1985–89

Architect-in-Charge: John Ike. Project Associate: Augusta Barone. Assistants: Charles Barrett, Grant Marani, Pat Tiné. Landscape Architect: Robert Ermerins. Landscape Assistant: Stephanie Abrams. Interior Design Associate: Lisa Maurer. Interior Design Assistant: Alice Yiu.

The American Houses of Robert A. M. Stern, with an introduction by Clive Aslet (New York: Rizzoli, 1991), 158–69.

Mildred F. Schmertz, "Palm Beach North," *House & Garden* 163 (July 1991): 112–19, 126.

Mecox Fields Lot 7
Bridgehampton, New York, 1986–89

Architect-in-Charge: Randy M. Correll. Assistant: Robert Demel.

Alastair Gordon, "A Place in the Sun," *On The Avenue* 3 (July/August 1987): 1, 4–6.

Julie V. Iovine, "Dawn of the New Old House," *Metropolitan Home* 21 (July 1989): 74–79.

Grand Harbor
Vero Beach, Florida, 1986–89

Architect-in-Charge: Paul L. Whalen. Assistants: John Berson, Christopher Blake, Sonia R. Cháo, Alexis O. Fernandez, Valerie Hughes, Michelle Huot, Warren A. James, Laurie D. Kerr, Daniel Lobitz, William C. Nolan, Karen Okazaki, Anthony Poon.

Michael deCourcy Hinds, "Florida Market: Ballyhoo and Bargains," *New York Times* (April 26, 1987), VIII: 1, 20.

Daralice D. Boles, "Resort Suburb by Robert Stern," *Progressive Architecture* 68 (July 1987): 41–42.

Philip Langdon, "A Good Place to Live," *Atlantic* 261 (March 1988): 39–60.

Thomas Fisher, "The New Urban Design," *Progressive Architecture* 69 (March 1988): 79–85.

Toshio Nakamura, "Recent Works of Robert A. M. Stern," *Architecture and Urbanism* 212 (May 1988): 128–35.

"File of Architect: Robert A. M. Stern Architects," *AT Architecture* (November 1988): 28–29.

Mitchell Rouda, "Builder's Choice," *Builder* 12 (October 1989): 134–39.

Lucia Funari, ed., *Robert A. M. Stern: Modernità e Tradizione* (Rome: Edizioni Kappa, 1990), 168–85.

Robert A. M. Stern: Selected Works, with an introduction by Charles Jencks (London: Academy Editions, 1991), 86–89.

Project of the Year Award, *Builder,* 1989; National Honor Award, American Institute of Architects, 1991.

Master Plan and Fine Arts Studio IV, Fine Arts Village, University of California, Irvine
Irvine, California, 1986–89

Architect-in-Charge: Graham S. Wyatt. Assistants: Preston J. Gumberich, Alexander P. Lamis, Jeff Schofield. Local Architect: The Lee/Naegle Partnership.

Toshio Nakamura, "Recent Works of Robert A. M. Stern," *Architecture and Urbanism* 212 (May 1988): 136–37.

Pilar Viladas, Susan Doubilet, "UC Builds," *Progressive Architecture* 69 (May 1988): 85–93.

Leon Whiteson, "A Campus by Design," *Los Angeles Times* (December 12, 1988), V: 1–3.

John Parman, "Utopia Revisited," *Architecture* 79 (January 1990): 66–69.

Robert A. M. Stern: Selected Works, with an introduction by Charles Jencks (London: Academy Editions, 1991), 84–85.

House at Wilderness Point
Fishers Island, New York, 1986–89

Architect-in-Charge: Randy M. Correll. Assistants: Yvonne Galindo, James Joseph. Landscape Architect: Robert Ermerins. Landscape Assistants: Stephanie Abrams, William C. Skelsey.

"Robert A. M. Stern Architects: House at Wilderness Point," *GA Houses* 28 (March 1990): 108–9.

The American Houses of Robert A. M. Stern, with an introduction by Clive Aslet (New York: Rizzoli, 1991), 146–57.

Clive Aslet, "Architecture: Robert A. M. Stern; Shingle Style Traditions for a New England Home" *Architectural Digest* 48 (July 1991): 88–95.

Excellence in Design Award, New York State Association of Architecture, American Institute of Architects, 1990.

Residence at Conyers Farm
Greenwich, Connecticut, 1986–89

Architect-in-Charge: Anthony Cohn. Project Manager: Elizabeth Valella. Assistants: Keller A. Easterling, Gary Tschirhart.

Meadowbrook II
Hempstead, New York, 1986–89

Architect-in-Charge: Barry Rice. Assistants: Adam Anuszkiewicz, Austin Brown, Michael D. Jones. Associated Architect: Brennan Beer Gorman/Architects.

Kathryn & Shelby Cullom Davis Hall, International House
500 Riverside Drive, New York, New York, 1987–89

Architect-in-Charge: Alexander P. Lamis. Senior Assistant: Pat Tiné. Assistants: Alexis O. Fernandez, Preston J. Gumberich

360 **Residence at Brainard Woods**
West Hartford, Connecticut, 1987–89

Architect-in-Charge: Joseph W. Dick. Assistants: Dierdre O'Farrelly, Jeff Schofield, Jay A. Waronker.

Casting Center, Walt Disney World
Lake Buena Vista, Florida, 1987–89

Architect-in-Charge: John Ike. Project Architect: Barry Rice. Assistants: Augusta Barone, Austin Brown, Luis Fontcuberta, Michael Jones, Scott Shin.

"File of Architect: Robert A. M. Stern Architects, 1983–1987," *AT Architecture* (November 1988): 30–31.

"In Progress," *Progressive Architecture* 69 (November 1988): 23, 39.

Patricia Leigh Brown, "In Fairy Dust, Disney Finds New Realism," *New York Times* (July 20, 1989), III: 1, 6.

Lynn Baxter, "It's Off to Work We Go," *Identity* 2 (Fall 1989): 36–41.

Paul M. Sachner, "Entertainment Architecture," *Architectural Record* 177 (September 1989): 66–71.

"Sticking with Stucco," *Architectural Record* 177 (December 1989): 186–87.

Nayana Currimbhoy, "A Touch of Magic," *Interiors* 150 (January 1990): 130–33.

Patricia Leigh Brown, "Disney Deco," *New York Times Magazine* (April 8, 1990): 18–22.

Paul Goldberger, "And Now, an Architectural Kingdom," *New York Times Magazine* (April 8, 1990): 23–24, edited extract reprinted as "Robert Stern: Disney Casting Center," in Dr. Andreas C. Papadakis, ed., *Post-Modernism on Trial* (London: Architectural Design, 1990), 60–65.

Paul Goldberger, "After Opulence, a New 'Lite' Architecture," *New York Times* (May 20, 1990), II: 1, 38.

Mark Alden Branch, "Why (and How) Does Disney Do It?" *Progressive Architecture* 71 (October 1990): 78–81.

Robert A. M. Stern: Selected Works, with an introduction by Charles Jencks (London: Academy Editions, 1991), 94–99, 137.

Janet Abrams, "The World According to Mickey," *Blueprint* 74 (February 1991): 28–35.

Kurt Andersen, "Look, Mickey, No Kitsch!" *Time* 138 (July 29, 1991): 66–69.

Best in General Office Design, 1990, *Interiors*.

Offices for Capitol Research Company
New York, New York, 1987–89

Architect-in-Charge: Alexander P. Lamis. Senior Assistant: Luis F. Rueda-Salazar. Assistants: Thai Nguyen, Jamshid Sepheri, Mary Ellen Stenger. Interior Design Associate: Raul Morillas. Interior Design Assistants: Deborah Emery, Stephan Johnson.

"Capital Gains," *Architectural Record* 177 (Mid-September 1988): 98–103. Award for Excellence in Planning and Design, *Architectural Record*, 1989; Lumen Award, New York Section, Illuminating Engineering Society, 1991.

Bancho House
Tokyo, Japan, 1988–89

Architect-in-Charge: Grant Marani. Assistants: W. David Henderson, Mabel O. Wilson. Interior Design Associate: Raul Morillas. Interior Design Assistants: Deborah Emery, Sharon Pett. Associated Architect: Kajima Corporation.

"File of Architect: Robert A. M. Stern Architects, 1983–1987," *AT Architecture* (November 1988): 34–35.

"In Progress," *Progressive Architecture* 69 (November 1988): 42.

Nora Richter Greer, "Americans Abroad: Some Coming Attractions," *Architecture* 78 (January 1989): 64–71.

Suzanne Stephens, "Have T Square: Will Travel," *Avenue* 14 (November 1989): 90–107.

Heidi Landecker, "Imperial Quarters," *Architecture* 79 (September 1990): 76–79.

Robert A. M. Stern: Selected Works, with an introduction by Charles Jencks (London: Academy Editions, 1991), 104–5, 130.

Akiko Busch, *Rooftop Architecture* (New York: Henry Holt and Company, 1991), 60–63.

Clare Melhuish, "Present Tense," *Building Design* (May 17, 1991): 20–21.

Bedford Garage
Farm Neck, Martha's Vineyard, 1988–89

Architect-in-Charge: Roger H. Seifter. Assistant: Michelle Huot.

Matanzas Shores Beach Club
Palm Coast, Florida, 1989

Architect-in-Charge: Paul L. Whalen. Project Associate: William C. Nolan.

City Hall Complex Competition
Orlando, Florida, 1989

Project Architect: Grant Marani. Assistant: Lee Ledbetter.

The Country Club and Houses for the Villages at Rocky Fork
New Albany, Ohio, 1989

Architect-in-Charge, Country Club: Paul L. Whalen. Architect-in-Charge, Villages: Stephen T. B. Falatko. Project Associate: William C. Nolan. Assistants: Christopher Blake, Richard Economakis, Alexis O. Fernandez, Preston J. Gumberich, Valerie Hughes, Michael D. Jones, Caryl Kinsey, Daniel Lobitz, Thai Nguyen, Edward H. A. Tuck, Rosamund Young, Lynn H. Wang, Jay A. Waronker.

Pierson Lakes Development
Sterlington, New York, 1989

Architect-in-Charge: Randy M. Correll.

Diana Shaman, "Using Architects' Designs to Sell Land," *New York Times* (January 12, 1990): 26.

"Architecture as a Merchandising Tool," *Architectural Record* 178 (April 1990): 27.

"Selling," *Builder* 13 (August 1990): 35.

Apartment Building, Surfer's Paradise
Queensland, Australia, 1989

Architects-in-Charge: Grant Marani, Barry Rice. Assistant: Michael D. Jones.

Morton Street Ventilation Building Competition
New York, New York, 1989

Architect-in-Charge: Steven T. B. Falatko. Assistants: E. J. Jarboe, Michael D. Jones, Robert Miller, Arthur Platt.

Roger Tory Peterson Institute
Jamestown, New York, 1989–

Architect-in-Charge: William T. Georgis. Project Associate: Laurie D. Kerr. Senior Assistant, Design Phase: Yvonne Galindo. Senior Assistant, Construction Documents Phase: Lynn H. Wang. Assistants: Ferenc Annus, Adam Anuszkiewicz, Augusta Barone, Silvina Geofron, Robert Han, Abigail M. Huffman, Arthur Platt, Paul Thompson, Elizabeth Valella. Landscape Architect: Robert Ermerins. Landscape Assistants: Laura H. Schoenbaum, William C. Skelsey.

Bed and Bath Furnishings for Atelier Martex
1989–

Architect-in-Charge: William T. Georgis. Senior Assistant: Andrew Zega.

Suzanne Slesin, "Classical Scenes on Sheets," *New York Times* (July 13, 1989), III: 3.

"Stern Builds A New Collection For WestPoint Pepperell," *LBD/Interior Textiles* (August 1989): 14.

"AD-At-Large: Architectural Linens," *Architectural Digest* 46 (December 1989): 236.

Charles Gandee, "Gandee At Large: Bob Stern Has a Dream," *House & Garden* 162 (January 1990): 150.

Arlene Hirst, "Hot Properties: Compromising Positions?" *Metropolitan Home* 22 (January 1990): 21.

Tommy Awards, American Printed Fabrics Council. For Newport Gardens and Pompeii, 1990.

Furniture for Hickory Business Furniture
1989–

Architect-in-Charge: William T. Georgis. Assistant: Sharon Pett.

"Stern Plans Furniture Production," *New York Times* (August 3, 1989), III: 3.

"Fax, Plans and Videotape," *Interiors* 138 (October 1989): 118–25.

"Hot Properties: Home from the Office," *Metropolitan Home* 21 (October 1989): 44.

"Products: Designer's Saturday's Star Productions," *Architecture* 78 (December 1989): 111–13.

Karen D. Stein, "Stern Stuff," *Architectural Record* 178 (January 1990): 159.

"Style Beat: Furnishing the Blueprint," *House Beautiful* 132 (January 1990): 16.

"Market: Robert Stern for HBF," *Interior Design* (January 1990): 80–81.

Nancy Crotti, "Architects, Designers Cater to Our Lust for Labels," *Asbury Park Press* (February 1, 1990), III: 1, 6.

"Showcase: Stern Seating," *Contract* (Canada) 9 (February/March 1990): 12.

Julie V. Iovine, "For Mining America's Memories," *Metropolitan Home* 22 (April 1990): 84, 158–59.

Jean Godfrey-June and Amy Milshtein, "Beyond Interior Design," *Contract Design* 33 (June 1991): 68–71.

Ziva Friedman, "Neocon 23: New Emphases Emerge," *Progressive Architecture* 72 (September 1991): 26.

Riverwalk, Chevron Land and Development Corporation
Mission Valley, San Diego, California, 1989–

Architect-in-Charge: Graham S. Wyatt. Assistants: Adam Anuszkiewicz, Preston J. Gumberich, Nancy K. Jordan, Elizabeth A. Kozarec, Sandra L. Parsons, Paul Thompson. Landscape Architect: Robert Ermerins. Landscape Assistant: Brian Sawyer. Associated Architects: Fehlman LaBarre Architects.

Concord Walk Hotel
Charleston, South Carolina, 1989–

Architect-in-Charge: Paul L. Whalen. Assistants: Daniel Lobitz, William C. Nolan. Architectural Advisor and Expeditor: Evans & Schmidt Architects.

Anglebrook Golf Club
Somers, New York, 1989–

Architect-in-Charge: Grant Marani. Senior Assistant: Gary Brewer. Assistants: Joseph Andriola, Lynn H. Wang.

Apartment House
Chicago, Illinois, 1989–

Architect-in-Charge: Alexander P. Lamis. Project Associate: William C. Nolan. Assistants: Daniel Lobitz, Rosamund Young. Landscape Architect: Robert Ermerins. Landscape Assistant: Laura H. Schoenbaum.

Fabric Design
Hickory Business Furniture, 1989–

Architect-in-Charge: William T. Georgis. Senior Assistant: Andrew Zega.

"AD-At-Large: Talking Textiles," *Architectural Digest* 48 (February 1991): 210.

Amy Gray Light, "Products: Woven from the Past," *Architecture* 80 (June 1991): 123.

Jean Godfrey-June and Amy Milshtein, "Beyond Interior Design," *Contract Design* 33 (June 1991): 68–71.

"Market: HBF Textiles," *Interior Design* 62 (July 1991): 42.

America House, The United States Embassy, Cultural and Consular Annex
Budapest, Hungary, 1989–

Architect-in-Charge: Graham S. Wyatt. Project Manager: Preston J. Gumberich. Assistants: Joseph Andriola, Ferenc Annus, Marina Annus, Peter Himmelstein, Adonica L. Inzer, Michael D. Jones, Elizabeth A. Kozarec, Kristin L. McMahon, Geoffrey P. Mouen. Associated Architect: KÖZTI.

Heidi Landecker, "Eastern Europe Offers Opportunities for Architects," *Architecture* 81 (February 1992): 27.

Carnegie Hill Townhouse
New York, New York, 1987–90

Architect-in-Charge, Design Phase: Alan J. Gerber. Architect-in-Charge, Construction Documents and Construction Phase: Roger H. Seifter. Project Associate: Kristin L. McMahon. Assistants: Augusta Barone, Michael Bolster, Mary Cerrone, Frank Weiner, Paul B. Williger. Landscape Architect: Robert Ermerins. Landscape Assistant: Stephanie Abrams.

Skyview
Aspen, Colorado, 1987–90

Architect-in-Charge: Armand LeGardeur. Senior Assistant: Derrick W. Smith. Assistants: Ferenc Annus, Mark Johnson, Karen E. Small. Landscape Architect: Robert Ermerins. Landscape Assistant: William C. Skelsey.

362 *The American Houses of Robert A. M. Stern,* with an introduction by Clive Aslet (New York: Rizzoli, 1991), 192–95.

Barbara Goldsmith, "Architecture, Robert A. M. Stern: Bold Forms on the Slope of Aspen's Red Mountain," *Architectural Digest* 49 (June 1992): 116–25.

Police Building
207 North Garfield Avenue, Pasadena, California, 1987–90

A Joint Venture with EKONA Ehrenkrantz/Kamages, Architects & Planners, San Francisco

Principals-in-Charge: Robert A. M. Stern, Christ J. Kamages. Project Manager: Timothy L. Craig. Project Architects: Karen Gibb, John Ike, Barry Rice. Project Team: Carlos Abruzzese, Augusta Barone, Austin Brown, Robin Burr, Warren A. James, Timothy E. Lenahan, Jane Marshall, Fakoor Popal, Michael Radcliffe, Jeff Schofield, Scott Shin.

"In Progress," *Progressive Architecture* 69 (November 1988): 42.

Marc Pally, "Conceiving a Courtyard," *Places* 6 (Spring 1990): 4–17.

Bill Tacy, *100 Contemporary Architects: Drawings and Sketches* (New York: Harry N. Abrams, 1991): 218–19.

Robert A. M. Stern: Selected Works, with an introduction by Charles Jencks (London: Academy Editions, 1991), 100–101.

Lynn Nesmith, "Law and Order," *Architecture* 80 (February 1991): 41–47.

Certificate of Excellence, AIA/ACA Architecture for Justice, 1991; Award of Merit, Golden Nugget Award, 1991.

Two Venture Plaza, Irvine Center
Irvine, California, 1988–90

Architects-in-Charge: John Ike, Thomas A. Kligerman, Barry Rice. Senior Assistant: Michael D. Jones. Associated Architect: Langdon Wilson Mumper Architects.

Robert A. M. Stern: Selected Works, with an introduction by Charles Jencks (London: Academy Editions, 1991), 106–7.

Ninety Tremont Street
Boston, Massachusetts, 1988–90

Architect-in-Charge: Ellen Kenyon Coxe. Project Associate: Thomas M. Eisele. Assistants: Michael Jones, Timothy E. Lenahan, Sandra L. Parsons. Associated Architect: Jung/Brannen Associates, Inc.

John King, "An Elegant Plea for Forbidden Boston Airspace," *Boston Globe* (February 11, 1989): 37.

Robert Campbell, "Tremont Temple's a Winner If Promises Are Kept," *Boston Globe* (May 15, 1990): 25, 32.

Herrmann Apartment
New York, New York, 1988–90

Project Manager: Elizabeth Valella. Interior Design Associate: Lisa Maurer. Interior Design Assistants: Nancy Boszhardt, Alice Yiu.

Residence at Cove Hollow Farm
East Hampton, New York, 1989–90

Architect-in-Charge: Randy M. Correll. Assistant: Daniel Romualdez.

Residence
Kiawah Island, South Carolina, 1989–90

Architect-in-Charge: Roger H. Seifter. Senior Assistant: John Berson.

Assistants: Christopher Blake, Daniel Romualdez. Landscape Architect: Robert Ermerins. Landscape Assistant: William C. Skelsey.

Residence
Bloomfield Hills, Michigan, 1989–90

Architect-in-Charge: Grant Marani. Senior Assistant: Lynn H. Wang. Assistant: Rosamund Young.

Alterations and Additions to the Edwards-Smyth House
Charleston, South Carolina, 1989–90

Architect-in-Charge: Roger H. Seifter. Project Associate: Augusta Barone. Assistant: Robert Miller. Landscape Architect: Robert Ermerins.

Pool and Pergola
Kiawah Island, South Carolina, 1989–90

Architect-in-Charge: Roger H. Seifter. Assistant: Derrick W. Smith. Landscape Architect: Robert Ermerins.

Kiawah Beach Club
Kiawah Island, South Carolina, 1989–90

Architect-in-Charge, Schematic Design Phase: Steven T. B. Falatko. Architect-in-Charge, Design Development and Construction Documents Phase: Roger H. Seifter. Project Associate: William C. Nolan. Assistants: Abigail M. Huffman, Diane J. Smith, Elizabeth Valella.

Washington State Labor and Industries Building Competition
Olympia, Washington, 1990

Architect-in-Charge: Stephen T. B. Falatko, Barry Rice. Senior Assistants: Michael Jones, Laurie D. Kerr, Lynn H. Wang. Assistant: E. J. Jarboe. Associated Architect: The Austin Company.

Espace Euro Disney
Villiers-sur-Marne, France, 1990

Architect-in-Charge: Paul L. Whalen. Assistant: Daniel Lobitz.

"Euro Disney Nouvelle Capitale du Rêve," *Paris Match* (December 13, 1990): I-XIII.

Janet Abrams, "The World According to Mickey," *Blueprint* 74 (February 1991): 28–35.

"Mass Observation: An American in Paris," *Sight and Sound* 1 (May 1991): 4–5.

Deborah Dietsch, "Mickey Goes to Paris," *Architecture* 81 (July 1992): 41–42.

Old Merchant's House Table Ornament
1990

Project Associate: Augusta Barone. Assistants: Kent Fikrig, Vincent Rose.

Del Mar Civic Center
Del Mar, California, 1990

Architect-in-Charge: Graham S. Wyatt. Senior Assistant: Joseph Andriola. Assistants: Austin Brown, Robert Ermerins, Preston J. Gumberich, Adonica L. Inzer, Laura H. Schoenbaum, Derrick W. Smith. Associated Architect: Bokal Kelley-Markham Architects.

Kay Kaiser, "Form Triumphs Over Substance and Del Mar is Poorer for It," *San Diego Union* (January 13, 1991), F: 1, 4.

Dirk Sutro, "A Good Idea that Needs Work," *Los Angeles Times* (April 25, 1991), E: 1, 11.

Dirk Sutro, "Del Mar Center is Elegant—but Flawed," *Los Angeles Times* (July 25, 1991), E: 1, 11.

Karen Salmon, "On The Boards: San Diego Area Developments," *Architecture* 80 (September 1991): 39.

Na Pali Haweo
Oahu, Hawaii, 1990–

Architect-in-Charge: Grant Marani. Assistants, houses: Joseph Andriola, Michael D. Jones, Nancy Jordan, Lynn H. Wang, Jay A. Waronker, Rosamund Young. Assistants, park: Joseph Andriola, Michael D. Jones, Nancy Jordan. Associated Architect: Johnson Tsushima Luersen Lowrey.

Disney Boardwalk Village and Hotel, Walt Disney World
Lake Buena Vista, Florida, 1990–

Architect-in-Charge: Paul L. Whalen. Hotel Project Manager: Alexander P. Lamis. Retail Project Manager: Daniel Lobitz. Senior Assistant: Gary Brewer. Assistants: David Biscaye, Victoria Delgado, N. Pablo Doval, Robert F. Epley, Charlotte M. Frieze, Adonica L. Inzer, Edward G. Kopel, Geoffrey P. Mouen, Jay A. Waronker. Landscape Project Manager: Robert Ermerins. Landscape Assistant: Brian Sawyer. Architect of Record: Morris Architects.

Chiburi Lake Golf Resort
Chiburi, Japan, 1990–

Architect-in-Charge: Grant Marani. Assistants: Michael D. Jones, Lynn H. Wang, Rosamund Young. Associated Architect: Kajima Corporation.

Kitsuregawa Golf Club House and Inn
Tochigi Prefecture, Japan, 1990–

Architect-in-Charge: Grant Marani. Senior Assistant: Joseph Andriola. Assistant, Club House: Nancy K. Jordan. Assistants, Inn: Jay Waronker, Rosamund Young. Associated Architect: Kajima Corporation.

"Architecture for Export," *Oculus* 53 (April 1991): 10.

West Village Golf Resort
Tochigi Prefecture, Japan, 1990–

Architect-in-Charge: Grant Marani. Senior Assistant: Joseph Andriola. Assistants: Victoria Delgado, Todd Fauser, Nancy K. Jordan, Rosamund Young, Adonica L. Inzer, Lynn H. Wang. Associated Architect: Matsuda Hirata & Sakamoto.

Clare Melhuish, "Present Tense," *Building Design* (May 17, 1991): 20–21.

Izumidai Resort
Izu Peninsula, Japan, 1990–

Architect-in-Charge: Grant Marani. Assistants: Joseph Andriola, Ferenc Annus, Gary Brewer, N. Pablo Doval, Peter Himmelstein, Adonica L. Inzer, Michael D. Jones, Nancy K. Jordan, Lee Ledbetter, Lynn H. Wang. Associated Architect: Kajima Corporation.

Residence at Briar Patch
East Hampton, New York, 1984–91

Architect-in-Charge: Randy M. Correll. Assistants: Kerry Moran, Jay A. Waronker. Landscape Architect: Robert Ermerins. Landscape Assistants: Charlotte M. Frieze, William C. Skelsey.

Ellen K. Popper, "Hamptons Houses Reverting to Traditional Style," *New York Times* (June 23, 1991), XII: 1, 6.

222 Berkeley Street
Boston, Massachusetts, 1986–91

Architects-in-Charge: Ellen Kenyon Coxe, Barry Rice. Project Associate: Thomas M. Eiselc. Design Phase Associates: Anthony Cohn, Timothy E. Lenahan. Assistants: Keller A. Easterling, Sandra L. Parsons, Elizabeth Valella. Associated Architects: Jung/Brannen Associates, Inc.; Kendall/Heaton Associates, Inc.

Geoffrey Rowan, "New Look Studied for N.E. Life," *Boston Herald* (January 18, 1987): 1, 109.

Robert Campbell, "Johnson's Boston Scheme Rejected; Developers Hire New Architect," *Architecture* 76 (March 1987): 38.

Robert A. M. Stern, *Modern Classicism* (New York: Rizzoli, 1988), 224, 226.

Robert Campbell, "Addressing Community Concerns Makes New Phase 2 a Triumph," *Boston Globe* (January 22, 1988): 1, 51.

Anthony J. Yudis, "A 'New' New England," *Boston Globe* (January 22, 1988): 1, 51.

Paul Goldberger, "A Tale of Two Towers On Boston's Boylston Street," *New York Times* (January 24, 1988): 31, 34.

Mark Muro, "The Architect as Superman," *Boston Globe* (February 5, 1988): 69–70.

Thomas Fisher, "P/A News Report: Public Presence in Boston," *Progressive Architecture* 69 (March 1988): 37–38.

Toshio Nakamura, "Recent Works of Robert A. M. Stern," *Architecture and Urbanism* 212 (May 1988): 138–39.

"File of Architect: Robert A. M. Stern Architects," *AT Architecture* (November 1988): 24–25.

Robert A. M. Stern, "Design as Emulation," in Dr. Andreas C. Papadakis, ed., *Imitation and Innovation* (London: Architectural Design, 1988): 20–24.

Heinrich Klotz, ed., *New York Architecture 1970–1990* (Munich: Prestel-Verlag, 1989), 316–17.

Teresa M. Hanafin and John King, "Lots & Blocks," *Boston Globe* (January 8, 1989), I: 73.

"The Buoyant Back Bay," *Boston Globe* (May 13, 1989): 41.

Lucia Funari, ed., *Robert A. M. Stern: Modernità e Tradizione* (Rome: Edizioni Kappa, 1990), 192–97.

Naomi Miller and Keith Morgan, *Boston Architecture 1975–90* (Munich: Prestel-Verlag, 1990), 152–53.

Robert A. M. Stern: Selected Works, with an introduction by Charles Jencks (London: Academy Editions, 1991), 90–93.

Robert Campbell, "Proper Bostonian," *Boston Globe* (November 1, 1991): 25, 33.

Robert Campbell, "A Logo of the Past on the Screen of the Present," *New York Times* (March 29, 1992), II: 38.

Ohrstrom Library, St. Paul's School
Concord, New Hampshire, 1987–91

Architect-in-Charge: Graham S. Wyatt. Project Managers: Preston J. Gumberich, Caryl Kinsey. Associate, Design Phase: Charles D. Warren. Assistants: Abigail M. Huffman, Timothy E. Lenahan, Sandra L. Parsons, Sharon Pett, Eva Pohlen, Mary Ellen Stenger. Landscape Architect: Robert Ermerins. Landscape Assistants: Laura H. Schoenbaum, William C. Skelsey. Interior Design Associate: Lisa Maurer. Interior Design Assistant: Alice Yiu.

"In Progress," *Progressive Architecture* 69 (November 1988): 40.

364   Lucia Funari, ed., *Robert A. M. Stern: Modernità e Tradizione* (Rome: Edizioni Kappa, 1990), 198–99.

Robert A. M. Stern: Selected Works, with an introduction by Charles Jencks (London: Academy Editions, 1991), 102–3.

Robert Campbell, "A Heavenly Library for a Few Privileged Readers," *Boston Globe* (May 14, 1991): 53, 56.

Robert Campbell, "Well-Schooled," *Architectural Record* 179 (August 1991): 56–63.

Paul Goldberger, "Enriching the Dialogue Between People and Books," *New York Times* (September 1, 1991), II: 24.

"Best of 1991 Design," *Time* 139 (January 6, 1992): 82.

Graham Wyatt and Rosemarie Cassels Brown, "A New Library for St. Paul's School," *School Library Journal* 38 (February 1992): 35–37.

Carter Wiseman, "Stern vs. Kahn in Preppieland," *New Criterion* 10 (March 1992), 62–64.

Distinguished Architecture Award, New York Chapter, American Institute of Architects, 1992.

Woodlynne
Birmingham, Michigan, 1987–91

Architect-in-Charge: Grant Marani. Senior Assistant: Rosamund Young. Assistants: W. David Henderson, Abigail M. Huffman, Lee Ledbetter, Luis F. Rueda-Salazar, Jay A. Waronker, Mabel O. Wilson.

Linda G. Byam, "Symphony Showhouse," *Birmingham-Bloomfield Lifestyle* (Spring–Summer 1989): 7–14.

"P/A News Report: Venturi Goes to Market," *Progressive Architecture* 70 (May 1989): 23, 30.

Carla Jean Schwartz, "The Articulate Architect," *Style* (Fall 1989): 58–63.

"Grand Award: Woodlynne," *Builder* 14 (October 1991): 117.

Gerald Frawley, "Just Grand: Builder's Classical House Earns Trade Magazine Award," *Building Scene* (October 13, 1991), VII: 1.

Grand Award, *Builder*, 1991.

Spruce Lodge
Old Snowmass, Colorado, 1987–91

Architect-in-Charge, Design and Construction Documents Phases: Thomas A. Kligerman. Architect-in-Charge, Construction Phase: Arthur D. Chabon. Assistants: Silvina Goefron, Abigail M. Huffman, Valerie Hughes, Timothy Haines, Leslie E. Mason, Robert Miller, Warren Van Wees, Andrew Zega. Landscape Design Associate: Robert Ermerins. Landscape Assistant: William C. Skelsey. Interior Design Associate: Raul Morillas. Interior Design Assistants: Nancy Boszhardt, Deborah Emery, Stephan Johnson, Paul C. McDonnell.

The American Houses of Robert A. M. Stern, with an introduction by Clive Aslet (New York: Rizzoli, 1991), 196–99.

Disney's Yacht and Beach Club Resorts, Walt Disney World
Lake Buena Vista, Florida, 1987–91

Architect-in-Charge: Alexander P. Lamis. Senior Assistant: Lynn H. Wang. Assistants: Christopher Blake, David J. Dwight, Richard Economakis, Robert Ermerins, Stephen T. B. Falatko, Alexis O. Fernandez, Preston J. Gumberich, Timothy E. Lenahan, John S. Mason, Thai Nguyen, Anthony Poon, Barry Rice, Jamshid Sepheri, Mary Ellen Stenger, Pat Tiné, Paul Williger. Concept and Schematic Planning: Hill Architects (formerly Frizzell Hill Moorhouse Architects). Architect of Record: VOA Associates, Inc.

Suzanne Stephens, "The Architectural Mouseketeers," *Avenue* 14 (December 1989): 106–15.

Charles Jencks, "Post-Modernism Between Kitsch and Culture," in Dr. Andreas C. Papadakis, ed., *Post-Modernism on Trial* (London: Architectural Design, 1990): 25–35.

Patricia Leigh Brown, "Disney Deco," *New York Times Magazine* (April 8, 1990): 18–22.

Mark Alden Branch, "Corporate Client Profile: Why (and How) Does Disney Do It," *Progressive Architecture* 71 (October 1990): 78–81.

Ross Miller, "Euro Disneyland and the Image of America," *Progressive Architecture* 71 (October 1990): 92–95.

Vincent Scully, "Animal Spirits," *Progressive Architecture* 71 (October 1990): 90–91.

Richard Sandomir, "Michael Eisner: The Man Behind the Magic at Disney," *Pinnacle* (January–February 1991): 8–13.

Janet Abrams, "The World According to Mickey," *Blueprint* 74 (February 1991): 28–35.

Chuck Twardy, "A Tale of Two Resorts," *Orlando Sentinel* (February 19, 1991), IV: 1,4.

David Dillon, "Disney's Grand Design," *Dallas Morning News* (February 24, 1991), III: 1, 8.

John Morris Dixon, "Editorial: Disney's World and Yours," *Progressive Architecture* 72 (April 1991): 9.

Claudine Mulard, "Le Monde Selon Disney," *Architecture Intérieur Créé* 242 (April/May 1991): 114–21.

Julie V. Iovine, "Metro: Disney's Sleeping Beauties," *Metropolitan Home* 23 (May 1991): 38.

Michael J. Crosbie, "Ace of Clubs," *Architecture* 80 (June 1991): 90–93.

Kurt Andersen, "Look, Mickey, No Kitsch!" *Time* 138 (July 29, 1991): 66–69.

Beverly Russell, "Fantasy on the Beach," *Interiors* 110 (October 1991): 56–59.

Marcus Binney, "Character Buildings," *Times Saturday Review*, London (March 7, 1992): 20–21.

The Town Square—Wheaton
Wheaton, Illinois, 1988–91

Architect-in-Charge: Graham S. Wyatt. Project Manager: Nancy K. Jordan. Assistants: Thomas M. Eisele, Timothy Haines, Sandra L. Parsons, Paul Thompson. Landscape Architect: Robert Ermerins. Landscape Assistant: Laura H. Schoenbaum.

Michael J. P. Smith, "Robert Stern Vs. Wayne's World," *Inland Architect* 34 (July/August 1990): 20, 22.

Jerry C. Davis, "Wheaton Getting 'Town Square' Mall," *Chicago Sun-Times* (February 4, 1991): 32.

David Young, "Shopping Takes Step into the Future," *Chicago Tribune* (March 2, 1992), XIX: 1, 5.

Robert Sharoff, "It Takes a Stern Hand to Be Whimsical," *Daily News Record* 22 (March 23, 1992): 28.

Neil Stern, "It's Not a Strip Center, Not a Regional Mall," *Crain's Chicago Business* (April 6, 1992), II: 18.

The Gables
Woodlynne, 1989–91

Architect-in-Charge: Grant Marani. Senior Assistant: Jay A. Waronker. Assistants: Joseph Andriola, W. David Henderson, Lee Ledbetter, Rosamund Young. Interior Design Associate: Raul Morillas. Interior Design Assistants: Deborah Emery, Stephan Johnson, Paul C. McDonnell, Leslie Radziemski.

Addition to a Cottage
East Hampton, New York, 1989–91

Architect-in-Charge: Randy M. Correll. Landscape Architect: Robert Ermerins. Assistant: William C. Skelsey.

Pool and Gazebo
Kiawah Island, South Carolina, 1990–91

Architect-in-Charge: Roger H. Seifter. Assistant: Elizabeth A. Kozarec. Landscape Architect: Robert Ermerins.

Banana Republic
744 North Michigan Avenue, Chicago, Illinois, 1990–91

Architect-in-Charge: Graham S. Wyatt. Project Manager: Lee Ledbetter. Senior Assistant: Derrick W. Smith. Assistant: Adonica L. Inzer. Landscape Architect: Robert Ermerins. Landscape Assistant: Laura H. Schoenbaum. Interior Design Associate: Raul Morillas. Interior Design Assistant: Nancy Boszhardt. Architect of Record: Robert W. Engel, Gap, Inc.

Sharon Stangenes, "A Stern View of the Jungle," *Chicago Tribune* (July 14, 1991): 2.

Genevieve Buck, "Bananas and Creme," *Chicago Tribune Style* (November 13, 1991), VII: 7–8.

"Banana Republic Stages Architectural Coup with New Store," *Chicago Sun-Times* (November 20, 1991), II: 1.

Paul Gapp, "Split Decision: Banana Republic Building Slips onto the Avenue," *Chicago Tribune* (December 22, 1991), XIII: 6–7.

"A Touch of Class for Casual Clothes," *Chicago* 41 (January 1992): 24.

"Architects as Decorators," *Oculus* 54 (January 1992): 10.

Philip Berger, "Top Banana," *Inland Architect* 36 (March/April 1992): 19, 22.

Robert Sharoff, "It Takes a Stern Hand to Be Whimsical," *Daily News Record* 22 (March 23, 1992): 28.

Arlene Hirst, "Hot Properties: Robert A. M. Stern's Top Banana," *Metropolitan Home* 24 (April 1992): 26.

The Turning Point Competition
Amstelveen, The Netherlands, 1990–91

Architect-in-Charge: Graham S. Wyatt. Senior Assistant: Joseph Andriola. Assistants: Adam Anuszkiewicz, Sandra L. Parsons, Lynn H. Wang, Rosamund Young.

Denver Public Library Competition
Denver, Colorado, 1990–91

Architect-in-Charge: Graham S. Wyatt. Project Associate: Alexander P. Lamis. Assistants: Joseph Andriola, Adam Anuszkiewicz, Augusta Barone, Austin Brown, Preston J. Gumberich, James Herman, Adonica L. Inzer, Daniel Lobitz, William C. Nolan, Lynn H. Wang, Rosamund Young, Andrew Zega. Associated Architect: Urban Design Group, Inc.

Tracy Seipel, "Architects Vie to Design $64 Million City Library," *Denver Post* (November 25, 1990), III: 1, 11.

Katharine Smith-Warren, "Civic Architecture Takes a Right Turn: Denver's Library Competition," *Competitions* 1 (Spring 1991): 12–17.

Karen Salmon, "Denver Library Competition," *Architecture* 80 (April 1991): 34.

Thomas Fisher, "Denver's New Library," *Progressive Architecture* 72 (May 1991): 28.

"New York: Yesterday, Today, and Tomorrow," Principal Parlor Room for Metropolitan Home Showhouse II
New York, New York, 1991

Architect-in-Charge: Kristin L. McMahon. Interior Design Associate: Raul Morillas. Interior Design Assistant: Witten R. Singer.

Patricia Dane Rogers, "Show House: When Artists Have Their Way," *Washington Post* (March 7, 1991): 18–19, 24–25.

Beth Sherman, "Multiple Personalities," *New York Newsday* (March 7, 1991): 79, 82–83.

Suzanne Slesin, "Non-Designer Show House to Toast Absent Friends," *New York Times* (March 7, 1991), III: 1, 6.

Craig Wilson, "Rooms for Improvement: Celebs Share Visions," *USA Today* (March 11, 1991), IV: 4.

"This Is the House That Love Built," *Newsweek* 117 (March 18, 1991): 51.

"Robert A. M. Stern—Architecture with a Human Face," *Metropolitan Home* 23 (September 1991): 60, 64, 69, 71, 82–85.

Disney Regional Shopping Center Competition
Orlando, Florida, 1991

Architect-in-Charge: Paul L. Whalen. Project Associates: Grant Marani, William C. Nolan. Senior Assistant: Sandra L. Parsons. Assistants: Adam Anuszkiewicz, N. Pablo Doval, Laura Schoenbaum, Elizabeth Valella, Rosamund Young.

Residence in Beverly Park
Beverly Hills, California, 1991

Architect-in-Charge: Armand LeGardeur. Assistants: Randy M. Correll, Daniel Romualdez. Landscape Architect: Robert Ermerins. Landscape Assistant: Charlotte M. Frieze.

Tivoli Museum and Apartments
Harajuku, Tokyo, Japan, 1991–

Architect-in-Charge: Grant Marani. Senior Assistants: Adam Anuszkiewicz, Derrick W. Smith, Rosamund Young. Assistants: Joseph Andriola, Ferenc Annus, Adonica L. Inzer, Mark Johnson, Geoffrey P. Mouen, William C. Nolan. Landscape Architect: Robert Ermerins. Associated Architect: Kengo Kuma & Associates.

Mountain Residence
Yamanashi Prefecture, Japan, 1991–

Architect-in-Charge: Grant Marani. Assistants: Adam Anuszkiewicz, Mark Johnson, Rosamund Young. Associated Architect: ASO's Design Mix.

Residence in Starwood
Aspen, Colorado, 1991–

Architect-in-Charge: Armand LeGardeur. Project Associate: Augusta Barone. Assistants: Adam Anuszkiewicz. Landscape Architect: Robert Ermerins. Landscape Assistant: Brian Sawyer.

366 **Brooks School Library**
North Andover, Massachusetts, 1991–

Architect-in-Charge: Graham S. Wyatt. Senior Assistant: Lee Ledbetter. Assistants: Joseph Andriola, Adonica L. Inzer, Derrick W. Smith. Landscape Architect: Robert Ermerins. Landscape Assistants: Charlotte M. Frieze, Brian Sawyer.

Residence in River Oaks
Houston, Texas, 1986–92

Architect-in-Charge: Roger H. Seifter. Project Managers, Scheme I: Peter Dick, Elizabeth Thompson. Project Manager, Scheme II: John Berson. Assistants, Scheme I: Richard Economakis, Michelle Huot, John S. Mason, Keith Moskow, Sharon Pett, Olivia Rowan. Assistants, Scheme II: Gary Brewer, Abigail M. Huffman, Kristin L. McMahon, Daniel Romualdez, Olivia Rowan. Landscape Architect: Robert Ermerins. Landscape Assistants: Laura H. Schoenbaum, William C. Skelsey. Interior Design Associate: Raul Morillas. Interior Design Senior Assistant: Patricia Burns. Interior Design Assistants: Paul C. McDonnell, Alice Yiu. Associated Architect: Richard Fitzgerald and Associates Architects.

The American Houses of Robert A. M. Stern, with an introduction by Clive Aslet (New York: Rizzoli, 1991), 62–67.

The Norman Rockwell Museum at Stockbridge
Stockbridge, Massachusetts, 1987–92

Architect-in-Charge: William T. Georgis. Project Associate: Augusta Barone. Senior Assistant: Derrick W. Smith. Assistants: Silvina Goefron, Michelle Huot, Michael D. Jones, Robert Miller, Edward H. A. Tuck, Elizabeth Valella. Landscape Architect: Robert Ermerins. Landscape Assistants: Laura H. Schoenbaum, William C. Skelsey.

Joseph Giovannini, "Currents: A New England Look for Norman Rockwell," *New York Times* (March 24, 1988), III: 3.

"Berkshire Classical: Stern Wins Norman Rockwell Museum Competition," *Architectural Record* 176 (April 1988): 61.

"Design: Stern Wins Limited Competition for Norman Rockwell Museum," *Architecture* 77 (April 1988): 44.

John Morris Dixon, "P/A News Report: Stern Wins Rockwell Museum," *Progressive Architecture* 69 (April 1988): 25–26.

"File of Architect: Robert A. M. Stern Architects, 1983–1987," *AT Architecture* (November 1988): 26.

Laurie Shaw, "Construction Phase Drawing Near for the New $7.2 Million Norman Rockwell Museum," *Berkshire Business Journal* (May 1990): 3.

Derek Gentile, "Rockwell Architect Plans 'Country Museum,'" *Berkshire Eagle* (June 18, 1990), II: 1, 2.

"New Museum for Rockwell," *New York Times* (May 12, 1991), X: 8.

"Cupola Tops Rockwell Museum," *Berkshire Eagle* (November 9, 1991), II: 1.

Abby Pratt, "Rockwell Sneak Preview," *Berkshire Eagle* ((June 22, 1992): 1, 4.

Abby Pratt, "Museum Exhibits, Photomurals to Trace the Life of Rockwell," *Berkshire Eagle,* (June 22, 1992): 4.

Euro Disney
Marne-la-Vallée, France, 1988–92

HOTEL CHEYENNE
Architect-in-Charge: Alexander P. Lamis. Architect-in-Charge, Conceptual Design Phase: Paul L. Whalen. Senior Assistant: Daniel Lobitz. Assistants: Christopher Blake, Keller A. Easterling, Warren A. James, Maria Resende.

Production Architect: Viguier, Jodry & Associés.

NEWPORT BAY CLUB HOTEL
Architect-in-Charge: Paul L. Whalen. Senior Assistants: Gary Brewer, Edward H. A. Tuck. Assistants: David Biscaye, N. Pablo Doval, Valerie Hughes, E. J. Jarboe, Edward G. Kopel, Geoffrey P. Mouen, Daniel Lobitz, Robert Miller, Willam C. Nolan. Production Architect: Michel Macary & Xavier Menu.

"Les Hôtels du Royaume de Mickey," *Le Moniteur* (July 1989): 61–66.

Jean-Pierre Cousin, "Cinq Hôtels pour Euro Disneyland," *Architecture Intérieure Créé* 230 (October/November 1989): 118–33.

Richard W. Stevenson, "Movie Theme Park Planned for Disneyland in France," *New York Times* (November 17, 1989), IV: 4.

Suzanne Stephens, "The Architectural Mouseketeers," *Avenue* 14 (December 1989): 106–15.

"Will 'Le Mickey' Play in Paris," *Places* 6 (Summer 1990): 89–91.

Charlotte Ellis, "Disney Goes to Paris," *Landscape Architecture* 80 (June 1990): 38–41.

Suzanne Stephens, "That's Entertainment," *Architectural Record* 178 (August 1990): 72–79, 121.

Fred A. Bernstein, ed., "Disney's Imagineer-in-Chief Tells All," *Metropolitan Home* 22 (October 1990): 85–86, 92–93.

Ross Miller, "Euro Disneyland and the Image of America," *Progressive Architecture* 71 (October 1990): 92–95.

"Euro Disney Nouvelle Capitale du Rêve," *Paris Match* (December 13, 1990): I-XIII.

Steven Greenhouse, "Playing Disney in the Parisian Fields," *New York Times* (February 17, 1991), III: 1, 6.

Barbara Rudolph, "Monsieur Mickey," *Time* 137 (March 25, 1991): 48–49.

Shaun Duncliffe, "History's Harvest," *Hotel Specification International* (Tunbridge Wells, Kent, England: Pennington Press, 1992), 12–13.

Richard Corliss, "Voilà! Disney Invades Europe. Will the French Resist?" *Time* 139 (March 20, 1992): 82–84.

Robert Stern, Interview by Wing Chao, *Connaissance des Arts* (April 1992, special issue): 36–45.

Philip Jodidio, "Euro Disney: Le Pari et le Rêve," *Connaissance des Arts* 482 (April 1992): 34–41.

Cathleen McGuigan, "Empire of the Fun," *Newsweek* 119 (April 13, 1992): 10–18.

John Rockwell, "Hotels as Well as Amusements Use Fantasy at Euro Disneyland," *New York Times* (April 14, 1992), III: 13.

"Robert A. M. Stern on Euro Disneyland," *Newsline* (Columbia University) (May/Summer 1992): 3, 6.

Paul Goldberger, "A Curious Mix of Versailles and Mickey Mouse," *New York Times* (June 14, 1992), II: 28–29.

Mildred F. Schmertz, "New Frontier: Hotel Cheyenne," *Architecture* 81 (July 1992): 52–53.

Mildred F. Schmertz, "Yankee Nostalgia: Newport Bay Club," *Architecture* 81 (July 1992): 54–57.

Residence in Hunting Valley
Geauga County, Ohio, 1990–92

Architect-in-Charge: Roger H. Seifter. Project Manager: John Berson. Senior

Assistant: Diane J. Smith. Assistants: Gary Brewer, Randy M. Correll, Abigail M. Huffman, Daniel Romualdez, Elizabeth Valella, Rosamund Young. Landscape Architect: Robert Ermerins. Landscape Assistant: Charlotte M. Frieze. Interior Design Associate: Raul Morillas. Interior Design Assistant: Paul C. McDonnell.

Darden School of Business, University of Virginia
Charlottesville, Virginia, 1992–

Architect-in-Charge: Graham S. Wyatt. Senior Assistant: Gary Brewer. Assistants: Joseph Andriola, Adam Anuszkiewicz, Augusta Barone, Adonica L. Inzer, Alexander P. Lamis, Rosamund Young, Andrew Zega. Landscape Architect: Robert Ermerins. Landscape Senior Assistant: Brian Sawyer. Landscape Assistant: Charlotte M. Frieze. Associated Architect: Ayers, Saint, Gross.

"Details," *Architecture* 81 (April 1992): 24.

Brooklyn Law School Tower
Brooklyn, New York, 1986–93

Architect-in-Charge: Paul L. Whalen. Project Architect: Barry Rice. Assistants: Ferenc Annus, Victoria Delgado, N. Pablo Doval, Thomas M. Eisele, Robert Han, Peter Himmelstein, Valerie Hughes, Warren A. James, Jeff Schofield. Associated Architects: Wank Adams Slavin Associates.

"Brooklyn Law School to Erect a $25M, 10–Story Addition," *New York Construction News* 38 (February 25, 1991): 1, 5.

Clare Melhuish, "Present Tense," *Building Design* (May 17, 1991): 20–21.

The Center for Jewish Life, Princeton University
Princeton, New Jersey, 1986–93

Architect-in-Charge: Alexander P. Lamis. Architect-in-Charge, Design Phase: Thomas A. Kligerman. Senior Assistant: Lee Ledbetter. Assistants: Peter Dick, Stephen T. B. Falatko, Alexis O. Fernandez, Preston J. Gumberich, Abigail M. Huffman, Valerie Hughes, Thai Nguyen, Arthur Platt, Elizabeth Thompson, Pat Tiné, Elizabeth Valella, Denise Wilson.

"For Architect Robert Stern, Center for Jewish Life is Small, but Tough, Project," *Princeton Today* (Spring 1988): 7.

Eric Thompson, "Building a Better University," *Nassau* (October 17, 1991): 10–11.

Phillip Arcidi, "Projects: Filling in Princeton," *Progressive Architecture* 73 (April 1992): 127–29.

Columbus Regional Hospital
Columbus, Indiana, 1988–93

Architect-in-Charge: Graham S. Wyatt. Project Manager: Austin Brown. Assistants: Ferenc Annus, Thomas Gay, Preston J. Gumberich, Timothy E. Lenahan, Sandra L. Parsons, Eva Pohlen, Mary Ellen Stenger, Elizabeth Thompson, Paul Thompson, Pat Tiné. Landscape Architect: Robert Ermerins. Landscape Assistants: Charlotte M. Frieze, William C. Skelsey. Interior Design Associates: Lisa Maurer, Raul Morillas. Interior Design Assistants: Alice Yiu, Patricia Burns. Associated Architect: The Falick/Klein Partnership, Inc.

Susan Ehlers, "Hospital Expanding into 21st Century," *Republic*, Columbus, Indiana (November 20, 1989): 1, 5.

Susan Ehlers, "Hospital Digs into the Future," *Republic*, Columbus, Indiana (April 6, 1990): 1.

"Equity, Justice and Architecture," *Interiors* 149 (May 1990): 205.

Susan Ehlers, "Hospital Gets Foundation Facelift," *Republic*, Columbus, Indiana (June 2, 1991), II: 1, 8.

Editorial, *Republic*, Columbus, Indiana (July 22, 1991): 6.

"Building Now for the 21st Century," *Republic*, Columbus, Indiana (October 6, 1991): special section insert.

"Outreach Critical to the Future," *Republic*, Columbus, Indiana (October 8, 1991): 4.

Susan Ehlers, "Prognosis: On Time; On Budget," *Republic*, Columbus, Indiana (October 23, 1991): 1.

"Hoosier Patron: Cummins Engine Foundation Continues to Foster Design in Columbus, Indiana," *Architecture* 79 (December 1990): 41.

"Robert A. M. Stern," *Newsline* (Columbia University) (December 1990/January 1991): 6.

William A. Orth, "Bartholomew County Hospital Undergoes Radical Surgery," *Construction Digest* 64 (March 4, 1991): 16–18.

House at Apaquogue
East Hampton, New York, 1989–93

Architect-in-Charge: Randy M. Correll. Senior Assistant: Daniel Romualdez. Assistants: Ferenc Annus, Gary Brewer. Landscape Architect: Robert Ermerins. Landscape Assistant: Charlotte M. Frieze.

Illustration Credits

The numbers below refer to page numbers, with figure numbers following in parentheses. For pages 340–51, the numbers within the parentheses refer to the order of the projects on the page, vertically 1 through 5, horizontally a and b. All photographs and drawings not credited below are by Robert A. M. Stern Architects.

Photography

Peter Aaron/ESTO: 18–19, 66–67, 70–71, 73, 77–79, 98–99, 102–3, 113–15, 141, 156, 158 (7, 10, 11), 159, 161–63, 180–91, 210–11, 214–19, 225–27, 230–35; © The Walt Disney Company: 146–47, 150–55; Used by permission of The Walt Disney Company: 204, 242–43, 246–47, 250–51, 253–55, 274 (1, 2), 278–79, 281–83.

Steven Brooke: 88–91; Courtesy of *Architectural Digest.* © 1990. All rights reserved: 34–35, 38–39, 42–43; Courtesy of *Architectural Digest.* © 1989. All rights reserved: 50–51, 53–57; Courtesy of *Architectural Digest.* © 1991. All rights reserved: 106–7, 109–11, 134–35, 137–39.

Richard Bryant: 142–43.

Louis Checkman: 164–65.

William Choi: 30–31, 63 (7, 8), 64–65.

Langdon Clay, Courtesy of *Metropolitan Home.* © 1989: 347 (4).

Whitney Cox: 45, 340 (2).

Mark Darley/ESTO: 33 (10), 121 (6), 122 (10, 11), 123 (14).

Derrick & Love: 74–75.

©The Walt Disney Company: 205–7.

Jesse Gerstein, Courtesy of *Elle Decor:* 200 (2).

Mick Hales: 203.

John Hall: 170–71, 285; Courtesy of *Metropolitan Home.* © 1991: 198–99.

Ted Hardin: 345 (4).

Harrington/Olson: 201.

Michael Hill: 344 (4).

Lizzie Himmel: 47 (3), 49.

Wolfgang Hoyt: 86.

Timothy Hursley: 258–59; 262–63; Courtesy of *House & Garden.* © 1991 by The Condé Nast Publications Inc.: 126–27, 130–31.

Ralph Hutchins: 340 (4).

Piet Janmaat: 321.

Balthazar Korab: 273.

Jane Lidz, Courtesy of *Architectural Digest.* © 1990. All rights reserved: 121 (5, 7), 122 (8, 9, 12, 13, 15).

Tony Macawile: 288–89.

Peter Mauss/ESTO: 157, 158 (8, 9), 346 (1).

Glen Calvin Moon: 237.

Omega Studios: 202 (16–18).

Cymie Payne: 63 (4).

Jock Pottle/ESTO: 306–7.

Robert Reck, Courtesy of *Architectural Digest.* © 1992. All rights reserved: 172–75, 178–79.

Steve Rosenthal: 21.

H. Durston Saylor. Used by permission of The Walt Disney Company: 275 (3, 4).

Beth Singer: 192–93, 238–39.

The SWA Group: 61.

Steve Turner: 125.

Peter Vitale. Courtesy of *Architectural Digest.* © 1987. All rights reserved: 22–23, 25.

Jurgen Wilhelm: 94, 95 (7, 9).

Renderings

F. M. Constantino: 257.

Al Forster: 348 (5b).

Hersey-Kyrk: 116 (9), 117 (10, 11).

John Mason: 28, 97, 104 (1), 105, 116 (7), 133, 194 (1), 195, 209, 221 (3) 273, 287, 289, 298 (2), 299, 303, 317, 325, 333, 343 (5a), 346 (5), 350 (1b, 5).

Thai Nguyen: 312 (5).

The SWA Group: 60.

Andrew Zega: 87, 104 (2), 119, 167 (3), 222 (1), 241, 270–71, 291, 294 (1), 295 (3), 311 (3), 312 (1), 314 (1), 315 (4), 318 (1), 322 (1), 326 (1, 2), 331, 335 (5, 7), 336, 337 (2), 338 (1), 339 (3), 347 (5b), 351 (1, 5).